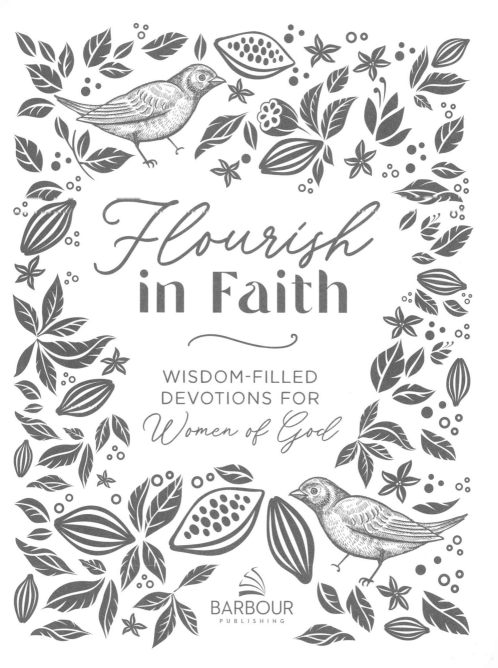

Flourish
in Faith

WISDOM-FILLED
DEVOTIONS FOR
Women of God

BARBOUR
PUBLISHING

Text previously appeared in *Daily Devotions for a Woman of Faith,* published by Barbour Publishing, Inc.

Print ISBN 978-1-63609-913-2

Scripture quotations marked KJV are taken from the King James Version of the Bible.

Scripture quotations marked NIV are taken from the HOLY BIBLE, NEW INTERNATIONAL VERSION®. NIV®. Copyright © 1973, 1978, 1984, 2011 by Biblica, Inc.™ Used by permission. All rights reserved worldwide.

Scripture quotations marked NLT are taken from the *Holy Bible.* New Living Translation copyright© 1996, 2004, 2015 by Tyndale House Foundation. Used by permission of Tyndale House Publishers, Inc. Carol Stream, Illinois 60188. All rights reserved.

Scripture quotations marked MSG are from *THE MESSAGE.* Copyright © by Eugene H. Peterson 1993, 1994, 1995, 1996, 2000, 2001, 2002. Used by permission of NavPress Publishing Group.

Scripture quotations marked AMPC are taken from the Amplified® Bible, Classic Edition, Copyright© 1954, 1958, 1962, 1964, 1965, 1987 by The Lockman Foundation. Used by permission.

Scripture quotations marked NCV are taken from the New Century Version of the Bible, copyright © 2005 by Thomas Nelson, Inc. Used by permission. All rights reserved.

Published by Barbour Publishing, Inc., 1810 Barbour Drive, Uhrichsville, Ohio 44683, www.barbourbooks.com

Our mission is to inspire the world with the life-changing message of the Bible.

Member of the
Evangelical Christian
Publishers Association

Printed in China.

Flourish in Faith

Do you desire to know God better? To be strengthened by Him? To see your faith grow more deeply rooted in Him and at the same time soar to new heights? Spending time with the Lord in prayer and Bible reading are the best ways to learn more about His mercy, His kindness, His love, and His peace.

These disciplines are like water on a sponge. They help us understand who God is and what He brings to our lives. In His presence, we become aware of His blessings and the resources He has provided to strengthen us for each day's battles. He will empower us to fulfill His plan for our lives.

It does take discipline to spend time with the Lord, but that simple discipline helps to keep our hope alive, providing light for our paths. When the schedule seems to loom large or the weariness of everyday living tempts you to neglect prayer and Bible study—remember they are your lifeline. They keep you growing in your relationship with your Father, Savior, and friend.

Blessed is the one. . .whose delight is in the law of
the LORD, and who meditates on his law day and night.
PSALM 1:1-2 NIV

Real Love

Beloved, let us love one another: for love is of God;
and every one that loveth is born of God, and knoweth God.
He that loveth not knoweth not God; for God is love.

1 JOHN 4:7–8 KJV

The world is full of counterfeits, but God's Word reveals the truth about love. The simple fact is that if we know God, we spend our lives loving Him. And the greatest way that we can love Him is by loving others. The apostle Paul tells us in 1 Corinthians that love is patient and kind. We can live with that. But then he gets to the part about not keeping a record of wrongs. . . Whoa, now that's a different story! What about severe offenses? We are supposed to just forgive and forget? What about our rights? Our boundaries? Isn't there a limit to how much an individual can forgive? The world says yes, but Jesus lived and taught the seventy-times-seven rule. Forgive again and again. Love relentlessly. Love is so much more than gifts or candy in a box. It endures. It stays the course. It keeps no record of wrongs.

Father, You love me with an unfailing love. You are incapable of anything less. May I reflect Your love to the world around me and to those who are closest in my life, especially to those who are close enough to hurt me. Amen.

Call Me

"Call on me in the day of trouble; I will deliver you, and you will honor me."
PSALM 50:15 NIV

"Call me and we'll do lunch."

"Call me and we'll talk more."

"Call if you need anything."

How many times have we said those words or heard them in return? Those two little words, *call me*, which hold such significance, have become so commonplace we barely think about them.

But when God says He wants us to call Him, He means it. He must lean closer, bending His ear, waiting, longing for the sound of His name coming from our lips. He stands ready to deliver us from our troubles or at least carry us through them safely.

David called on God in his troubles. Some of those troubles were of David's own making, while others were out of his control. It's a good thing God doesn't distinguish between the troubles we deserve and those we don't deserve. As far as He's concerned, we're His children. He loves us, and He wants to help us any way He can.

While He doesn't always choose to fix things with a snap of His fingers, we can be assured that He will see us through to the other side of our troubles by a smoother path than we'd travel without Him. He's waiting to help us. All we have to do is call.

Dear Father, I'm so glad I can call on You
anytime, with any kind of trouble. Amen.

Encourage One Another

So encourage each other and build each other up, just as you are already doing.
1 Thessalonians 5:11 nlt

. . . .

Encouragement means literally to "put courage in." When you encourage others, you are putting courage into their hearts. Christ calls us to encourage one another. This does not mean just to offer compliments or utter overused phrases in times of trouble such as, "It will all be okay," or "I hope it all works out." Biblical encouragement means instilling in someone's heart the courage needed to face the world. The Greek root word translated "encourage" in the New Testament is *paracollatos*, the verb form of the noun *paraclete*. *Paraclete* means "to lay alongside." We are called to come alongside those in need and encourage them. Just as the Holy Spirit encourages our hearts, we can affirm others. Try to focus your encouragement on the person and not anything they have done. Build them up. Speak words of truth into their life. Steer clear of empty compliments or forms of encouragement that rely on actions. Try, "I believe in you. God will be faithful to complete the good work He has begun," or "I really appreciate who you are."

When you need encouragement, does it sometimes seem that no one is there to offer it? Simply ask the Holy Spirit to draw near to you. He is your comforter, sent by the Lord to strengthen and guide you.

Lord, I want to put courage into others' hearts. Amen.

Talk to Your Best Friend

God is faithful, who has called you into fellowship
with his Son, Jesus Christ our Lord.
1 Corinthians 1:9 niv

When do you pray? How often do you call on God? Where do you talk to Him?

Just as we converse with our husband or best friend about what's happening in our lives, the Lord expects and anticipates conversations with us too.

Yes, He knows all about us, but He desires our fellowship one-on-one. Jesus chose twelve disciples with whom to fellowship, teach, and carry His message to every nation. They lived and ate with Jesus; they knew Him personally; they were His best friends. In the same manner, God gives us the divine privilege to know Him on a personal level through our relationship with Christ.

When, where, or how we talk to God is of little importance to the Savior. We can converse with the Lord while driving to work, walking through the park, or standing at the kitchen sink. We can ask for His help in the seemingly insignificant or in bigger decisions. Our concerns are His concerns too, and He desires for us to share our heartfelt thoughts with Him.

Fellowshipping with God is talking to our best friend, knowing He understands and provides help and wisdom along life's journey. It's demonstrating our faith and trust in the one who knows us better than anyone.

Lord, remind me to talk to You anytime, anywhere.
I know that as I pray, You will talk to me too. Amen.

8

Climbing Mountains

The LORD is my light and my salvation—whom shall I fear?
The LORD is the stronghold of my life—of whom shall I be afraid?
PSALM 27:1 NIV

. . . .

The Meteora in Greece is a complex of monastic structures high atop a mountain. Access to the structures was deliberately difficult. Some of these "hanging monasteries" were accessible only by baskets lowered by ropes and winches, and to take a trip there required a leap of faith. An old story associated with the monasteries said that the ropes were only replaced "when the Lord let them break."

While most of us will probably never scale the mountain to visit these monasteries, we often feel that we have many steep mountains of our own to climb. Maybe there's too much month at the end of the money. Or it could be health or relationship troubles. Whatever the reason we are hurting, angry, or feeling despair or hopelessness, God is ready to help us, and we can place all our hope in He who is faithful. We can do that because we are connected to Him and have seen His faithfulness in the past.

Lord, I will stay strong in You and will take courage. I can trust and rest in You. Whatever I am feeling now, whatever emotions I have, I give them to You, for You are my hope and salvation. You are good all the time, of which I can be supremely confident. Amen.

Stop Pretending

Don't just pretend to love others. Really love them.
ROMANS 12:9 NLT

Many times in our lives we are hurt deeply by those closest to us. And because they are family members or people that we must maintain a relationship with, we pretend to love them by sweeping issues under the rug. We go through the motions of relating to them in peace while nursing bitterness in our hearts. Mother Teresa said, "If we really want to love we must learn how to forgive."

God wants our relationships to be real. He wants us to be real with Him and real with others. Pretending is being dishonest. He says in Matthew 15:7–8 that the religious leaders honored Him with their lips, but their hearts were far from Him. He calls them hypocrites.

Are you hypocritical in your close relationships? Are you pretending to love when you feel nothing even close?

Tell the Lord how you feel. Ask for His help to overcome your fear of sharing your heart and being real with Him and others. Learn how to forgive, and watch as the Lord transforms your relationships into something that honors Him.

Heavenly Father, help me overcome my fear of sharing
my true feelings. Forgive me for pretending to love
when my heart is not in it. I want to live in authentic
relationship with You and with those I love. Amen.

Promises of God

"For the LORD your God is living among you. He is a mighty savior.
He will take delight in you with gladness. With his love, he will
calm all your fears. He will rejoice over you with joyful songs."
ZEPHANIAH 3:17 NLT

Look at all the promises packed into this one verse of scripture! God is with you. He is your mighty savior. He delights in you with gladness. He calms your fears with His love. He rejoices over you with joyful songs. Wow! What a bundle of hope is found here for the believer. Like a mother attuned to her newborn baby's cries, so is your heavenly Father's heart for you. He delights in being your Father. He knows when the storms of life are raging all around you. He senses your need to be held close and for your fears to be calmed. It is in those times that He is for you a Prince of Peace, a comforter. He rejoices over you with joyful songs. Can you imagine that God loves you so much that you cause Him to sing? God sings over you. And the songs He sings are joyful. He loves you with an unconditional, everlasting love. Face this day knowing that your God is with you. He calms you. And He sings over you. You are blessed to be a daughter of the King.

Father, thank You for loving me the way
You do. You are all I need. Amen.

Put on Love

And over all these virtues put on love,
which binds them all together in perfect unity.
COLOSSIANS 3:14 NIV

How many mornings have we stood in our closets, looking hopelessly at its overstuffed contents and thinking we have nothing to wear? What we're really thinking is that we have nothing to wear that makes us feel cute or pretty or sporty or professional—or whatever look we're going for that day. We want to look attractive. We want others to be drawn to us. And sometimes, no matter how many outfits we have to choose from, nothing feels right.

But there is one accessory we all have available to us that always fits. It always looks right, is always appropriate, and always makes us more attractive to others. When we wear it, we are beautiful, no matter how faded or dated our wardrobes may be. When we wear it, we become more popular, more sought after, more admired.

What is that accessory, you ask, and where can you buy it?

It's love, and you can't buy it anywhere. But it's free, and it's always available through the Holy Spirit. When we call on Him to help us love others, He cloaks us in a beautiful covering that draws people to us and makes us perfectly lovely in every way.

Dear Father, as I get dressed each day, help me to remember
the most important accessory I can wear is Your love. Amen.

Focused Prayer

*Pray in the Spirit at all times and on every occasion. Stay alert and
be persistent in your prayers for all believers everywhere.*
EPHESIANS 6:18 NLT

"Turn your eyes upon Jesus. Look full in His wonderful face. And the things of earth will grow strangely dim in the light of His glory and grace." It is an old hymn that has been sung for generations, but its words still ring true today. The Bible warns us to stay alert and to pray persistently. The key is to focus on Jesus even in the midst of the storm. If the captain of a ship or the pilot of a plane loses focus in the middle of a storm, it can be very dangerous for all involved. Our job as believers is to trust the Lord with the outcome and to remain deliberate and focused in our prayers.

The Bible doesn't say to pray when it is convenient or as a last resort. It doesn't say to pray *just in case* prayer might work or to add prayer to a list of other things we are trying. We are instructed in Ephesians to *pray at all times* and on *every occasion*. When you pray, pray in the Spirit. Pray for God's will to be done. Pray in the name of Jesus. There is great power in focused prayer.

Jesus, I set my eyes upon You, the Messiah,
my Savior, redeemer, and friend. Amen.

I Give Up

God so loved the world that he gave his one and only Son,
that whoever believes in him shall not perish but have eternal life.
JOHN 3:16 NIV

God encourages us to surrender to Him. How does God expect us to do that? *Merriam-Webster* defines *surrender* as "to give (oneself) over to something (as an influence)." God has given us free will, so the choice becomes ours: to surrender or maintain total control.

When we make the decision to surrender, we give ourselves over to God and allow His authority in our lives. We place our hope in the God who runs the universe. Oswald Chambers said, "The choice is either to say, 'I will not surrender,' or to surrender, breaking the hard shell of individuality, which allows the spiritual life to emerge."

Isn't that an amazing thought? Our Creator God cares enough about us to delve into our everyday lives and help us. Through the Holy Spirit within, God's gentle hand of direction will sustain each of us, enabling us to grow closer to our Father. The closer we grow, the more like Him we desire to be. Then His influence spreads through us to others. When we surrender, He is able to use our lives and enrich others. What a powerful message: give up and give more!

Lord, thank You for loving us despite our frailties.
What an encouragement to me today. Amen.

Open the Book

*For everything that was written in the past was written to teach
us, so that through the endurance taught in the Scriptures and
the encouragement they provide we might have hope.*
ROMANS 15:4 NIV

. . . .

"Out with the old and in with the new!" is unfortunately some Christians'
philosophy about the Bible. Yet the Old Testament scriptures are vital to
every believer. We cannot understand the power of the New Testament until
we embrace the teachings, wisdom, and moral laws of God revealed in the
Old Testament. After all, the Old Testament points directly to the coming
of the Messiah, Jesus, and our salvation.

The apostle Paul reminds us that everything in the Bible was written
with purpose—to teach us that through our trials and the encouragement
of God's Word we might have hope.

Life is tough, after all. We get discouraged and, at times, disheartened
to the point of such despair it's hard to recover. Yet the Word of God ignites
the power of a positive, godly fire within.

Reading *all* of God's Word is paramount. It is the source of hope, peace,
encouragement, salvation, and so much more. It moves people to take
action while diminishing depression and discouragement. As the writer of
Hebrews put it, "For the word of God is alive and active. Sharper than any
double-edged sword." (Hebrews 4:12 NIV).

Need some encouragement? Open the Book.

Lord, help me read Your Word consistently to empower
me with the hope and encouragement I need. Amen.

Feeling safe
and secure rests
not in the world
or in other human
beings but with
God alone.

What If?

The LORD will keep you from all harm—he will watch over your life.
PSALM 121:7 NIV

. . . .

"Mommy, what if the sun falls down? What if an earthquake swallows our house? What if. . .?" When the world appears scary to children, they run to their parents with questions. They look to their mothers and fathers for comfort, reassurance, and peace.

Grown-ups are no different. They run to Father God with their what-ifs. "What if I have cancer? What if I lose my job? What if there is a terrorist attack? What if. . . ?"

Psalm 46 provides the answer to all these questions. It says, "God is our refuge and strength, an ever-present help in trouble. Therefore we will not fear, though the earth give way and the mountains fall into the heart of the sea, though its waters roar and foam and the mountains quake with their surging. . . . The LORD Almighty is with us; the God of Jacob is our fortress" (vv. 1–3, 7 NIV).

Feeling safe and secure rests not in the world or in other human beings but with God alone. He is a Christian's help and hope in every frightening situation. He promises to provide peace to all who put their faith and trust in Him.

What are you afraid of today? Allow God to encourage you. Trust Him to bring you through it and to give you peace.

Dear Lord, hear my prayers, soothe me with
Your words, and give me peace. Amen.

His Steady Hand

The LORD makes firm the steps of the one who delights in him; though he may stumble, he will not fall, for the LORD upholds him with his hand.

PSALM 37:23–24 NIV

The wonderful thing about our mighty God is He knows our hearts. There are days when we succumb to responding or acting out in the flesh. But praise God, He loves us so much and is faithful even when we as human beings are unable to be. Just as a parent grasps a child's hand, He will take ours in His and help us along our pathway.

The Lord knows there are times when we will stumble. We may even backslide into the very activity that caused us to call on the Lord for salvation in the first place. But His Word assures us His love is eternal, and when we cry out to Him, He will hear.

Do not be discouraged with those stumbling blocks in your path, because the Lord is with you always. Scripture tells us we are in the palm of His hand. Hope is found in the Lord. He delights in us and wants the very best for us because of His perfect love.

Lord God, the cross was necessary for sinners like me.
I thank You that You loved me enough to choose me,
and that I accepted the free gift of salvation. Amen.

Working Hard

Whatever you do, work at it with all your heart,
as working for the Lord, not for human masters.
COLOSSIANS 3:23 NIV

Paul encouraged his readers to work hard, with all their hearts. Many of the new converts were enslaved to non-Christian masters. The tension between Christians and non-Christians increased when the non-Christian had the authority to lord it over the Christian.

But the wisdom in this verse applies to us today. We should always work hard, always give our best, even if we don't like our bosses. Ultimately, the quality of work we do reflects on our Father. If we're lazy or if our work is below standard, it has a negative impact on the body of Christ. But when we meet our deadlines and our work exceeds expectations, we give others a positive impression of what it means to be a Christian.

If we want to get ahead in our jobs and we want to help build the kingdom of God, we must have impeccable reputations. One way to build a positive reputation is to be a hard worker. When we do our absolute best at any task, people notice. When we consistently deliver quality products and services, people notice. We honor God and we honor ourselves when we work hard at the tasks we've been given.

Dear Father, I want to honor You with the work I do.
Help me to work hard, with all my heart. Amen.

I Forgive You

Smart people know how to hold their tongue;
their grandeur is to forgive and forget.
PROVERBS 19:11 MSG

. . . .

Great power comes in these three little words: *I forgive you.* Often they are hard to say, but they are powerful in their ability to heal our own hearts. Jesus taught His disciples to pray, "Forgive us our trespasses as we forgive those who trespass against us." He knew we needed to forgive others to be whole. When we are angry or hold a grudge against someone, our spirits are bound. The release that comes with extending forgiveness enables our spirits to commune with God more closely, and love swells within us.

How do you forgive? Begin with prayer. Recognize the humanity of the person who wronged you, and make a choice to forgive. Ask the Lord to help you forgive the person. Be honest, for the Lord sees your heart. Trust the Holy Spirit to guide you and cleanse you. Then step out and follow His leading in obedience.

By forgiving, we can move forward, knowing that God has good things in store for us. And the heaviness of spirit is lifted, and relief washes over us after we've forgiven. A new sense of hope and expectancy rises. *I forgive you.* Do you need to say those words today?

Father, search my heart and show me areas where I might need to forgive another. Help me let go and begin to heal. Amen.

Get Above It All

Set your minds and keep them set on what is above
(the higher things), not on the things that are on the earth.
COLOSSIANS 3:2 AMPC

If you've ever flown in an airplane, you know with one glimpse from the window at thirty thousand feet how the world seems small. With your feet on the ground, you may feel small in a big world; and it's easy for the challenges of life and the circumstances from day to day to press in on you. But looking down from above the clouds, things can become clear as you have the opportunity to get above it all.

Sometimes the most difficult challenges you face play out in your head—where a struggle to control the outcome and work out the details of life can consume you. Once removed—far away from the details—you can see things from a higher perspective. Close your eyes and push out the thoughts that try to grab you and keep you tied to the things of the world.

Reach out to God and let your spirit soar. Give your concerns to Him and let Him work out the details. Rest in Him and He'll carry you above it all, every step of the way.

God, You are far above any detail of life that concerns me. Help me to trust You today for answers to those things that seem to bring me down. I purposefully set my heart and mind on You today. Amen.

Answer Me!

Answer me when I call to you, my righteous God. Give me relief
from my distress; have mercy on me and hear my prayer.
PSALM 4:1 NIV

Have you ever felt like God wasn't listening? We've all felt that from time to time. David felt it when he slept in a cold, hard cave night after night, while being pursued by Saul's men. He felt it when his son Absalom turned against him. Time and again in his life, David felt abandoned by God. And yet, David was called a man after God's own heart.

No matter our maturity level, there will be times when we feel abandoned by God. There will be times when our faith wavers and our fortitude wanes. That's okay. It's normal.

But David didn't give up. He kept crying out to God, kept falling to his knees in worship, kept storming God's presence with his pleas. David knew God wouldn't hide His face for long, for he knew what we might sometimes forget: God is love. He loves us without condition and without limit. And He is never far from those He loves.

No matter how distant God may seem, we need to keep talking to Him. Keep praying. Keep pouring out our hearts. We can know, as David knew, that God will answer in His time.

Dear Father, thank You for always hearing my prayers.
Help me to trust You, even when You seem distant. Amen.

A Choice

*I'm singing joyful praise to G*OD*. I'm turning cartwheels of joy to my Savior God. Counting on G*OD*'s Rule to prevail, I take heart and gain strength. I run like a deer. I feel like I'm king of the mountain!*
HABAKKUK 3:18–19 MSG

. . . .

Many days, life seems like an uphill battle, where we are fighting against the current, working hard to maintain our equilibrium. Exhausted from the battle, it's tempting to throw up our hands in disgust and quit. That's when we should realize we have a choice. We can choose to surrender our burdens to the Lord!

What would happen if we followed the example in Habakkuk 3 and turned a cartwheel of joy in our hearts—regardless of the circumstances— then leaned in and trusted His rule to prevail? Think of the happiness and peace that could be ours with a total surrender to God's care.

It's a decision to count on God's rule to triumph. And we must realize His Word, His rule, never fails. Never. Then we must want to stand on that Word. Taking a giant step, armed with scriptures and praise and joy, we can surmount any obstacle put before us, running like a deer, climbing the tall mountains. With God at our side, it's possible to be king of the mountain.

Dear Lord, I need Your help. Gently guide me so I might learn
to lean on You and become confident in Your care. Amen.

The Lord Himself Goes before You

"The LORD himself goes before you and will be with you; he will never leave you nor forsake you. Do not be afraid; do not be discouraged."
DEUTERONOMY 31:8 NIV

How comforting and freeing it is when we allow God to go before us! Stop and consider that for a moment: you can relinquish control of your life and circumstances to the Lord Himself. Relax! His shoulders are big enough to carry all of your burdens.

The issue that has your stomach in knots right now? Ask the Lord to go before you. The problem that makes you wish you could hide under the covers and sleep until it's all over? Trust that God Himself will never leave you and that He is working everything out.

Joshua 1:9 (NIV) tells us to "be strong and courageous. Do not be afraid; do not be discouraged, for the LORD your God will be with you wherever you go." Be encouraged! Even when it feels like it, you are truly never alone. And never without access to God's power.

If you've trusted Christ as your Savior, the Spirit of God Himself is alive and well and working inside you at all times. What an astounding miracle! The Creator of the universe dwells within you and is available to encourage you and help you make right choices on a moment-by-moment basis.

Thank You, Lord, for the incredible gift of Your presence in each and every situation I face. Allow me to remember this and to call upon Your name as I go about each day. Amen.

Jonah's Prayer

"When my life was ebbing away, I remembered you, LORD,
and my prayer rose to you, to your holy temple."

JONAH 2:7 NIV

. . . .

Jonah ran from God. He knew where God had directed him to go, but he refused. He thought he knew better than God. He trusted in his own ways over God's. Where did it get him? He ended up in the belly of a great fish for three days. This was not a punishment but rather a forced retreat! Jonah needed time to think and pray. He came to the end of himself and remembered his Sovereign God. He describes the depths to which he was cast. This was not just physical but emotional as well. Jonah had been in a deep struggle between God's call and his own will.

In verse 6 of his great prayer from the belly of the fish, we read these words: "But you, LORD my God, brought my life up from the pit." When Jonah reached a point of desperation, he realized that God was his only hope. Have you been there? Not in the belly of a great fish, but in a place where you are made keenly aware that it is time to turn back to God? God loves His children and always stands ready to receive us when we need a second chance.

Father, like Jonah I sometimes think my own ways
are better than Yours. Help me to be mindful that
Your ways are always good and right. Amen.

How Great Is Our God!

And I said, O Lord God of heaven, the great and terrible
God, Who keeps covenant, loving-kindness, and mercy for
those who love Him and keep His commandments.
NEHEMIAH 1:5 AMPC

When Dorothy finally met the wizard she had been searching for in *The Wonderful Wizard of Oz*, she was disappointed. The "great and terrible" magician, who had propped himself up as an all-powerful man with a short temper, turned out to be a normal person behind a curtain—albeit one who was good at special effects.

Rest assured, when we finally meet God, we won't experience this type of letdown. The Bible notes God's inestimable qualities—unconditional love, unending mercy, unimaginable strength—with reverence. The New Testament authors also repeatedly wrote about God's mercy and compassion. He is a fully approachable God!

Of course, we need to fear and respect the holy Creator and Maker of all things and strive to do His will, but as the one who formed us, God knows that we will fail (and loves us anyway). His love is why He sent Jesus to die on the cross.

Today, think about God's love, mercy, and strength as you go about your routine. When you face problems, ask Him to solve them, instead of trying to fix them yourself. Repeatedly and reverently surrender to Him—because He is great, but He's certainly not terrible.

Creator, Maker, Redeemer God–You are wonderful.
Thank You for Your wisdom, strength, and love. Amen.

God's Love Song

"The LORD your God is with you, the Mighty Warrior who saves. He will take great delight in you; in his love he will no longer rebuke you, but will rejoice over you with singing."

ZEPHANIAH 3:17 NIV

Read Zephaniah 3:17, and you will find a verse packed with God's love. First, this verse reminds God's children that He is always with them. Wherever they go, whatever they do, in every situation, God watches over them with Fatherly love. Next, it says that God's love is not just ever-present but also all-powerful. When bad things happen, God's children needn't ask, "Where is God?" They can be confident that their Father is present with a mighty plan to save them. The verse continues, conveying God's gentleness in love. He quiets His children. His love is like a soft, soothing lullaby sung by a mother to her child. It brings His children comfort and peace. The verse ends with God singing. Yes, God sings! The Bible says in Zephaniah 3:17 that God rejoices over His children with singing. Isn't that amazing? God takes such delight in His children that He cannot contain His love for them. His love bursts forth in joyous song.

From beginning to end, this little piece of scripture is God's love song to His children. You are His child. Read it often, and know that He loves you.

Dear God, thank You for loving me fully,
unconditionally, and always. Amen.

Open the Eyes of Faith

*"Therefore I tell you, whatever you ask for in prayer,
believe that you have received it, and it will be yours."*
MARK 11:24 NIV

. . . .

At the conclusion of World War II and the end of the Holocaust, these words were found scratched on the wall of an abandoned farmhouse: "I believe in the sun even when it does not shine. I believe in love, even when it is not shown. I believe in God, even when He is silent." Sketched alongside the timeworn prose was the Star of David.

Have you ever prayed for something or someone, and God seemed to turn a deaf ear? One woman prayed for her son's salvation for seven years. Each day she knelt at the foot of her tearstained bed, pleading for her child. But God seemed silent. Yet, what she failed to understand was that the Lord had been working all along to reach her son in ways unknown to her. And finally her son embraced the gospel through a series of life-changing circumstances.

The world says, "I'll believe it when I see it," while God's Word promises, "Believe then see."

Someone once said, "The way to see by faith is to shut the eye of reason." When we pray, rather than ask God why our prayers remain unanswered, perhaps we should ask the Lord to close our eyes so that we might see.

Lord, I believe, even when my prayers go unanswered.
Instead, I know You are at work on my behalf. Amen.

The world says,
"I'LL BELIEVE IT
WHEN I SEE IT,"
while God's
Word promises,
"BELIEVE THEN SEE."

Love Leads the Way

*"You yourselves have seen what I did to Egypt, and how I
carried you on eagles' wings and brought you to myself."*
EXODUS 19:4 NIV

. . . .

When Moses led the children of Israel out of Egypt toward the Promised Land, he did not take them on the shortest route. God directed him to go the long way lest the people turn back quickly when things became difficult. God led them by day with a pillar of clouds and by night with a pillar of fire. How clearly He showed Himself. The people placed their hope in an almighty God and followed His lead. When they were thirsty, God gave water. When they were hungry, He sent manna. No need was unmet.

The amount of food and water required for the group is unimaginable. Moses depended on God. He believed God would care for them because he knew of God's great love and trusted in the Creator.

If God can do this for so many, do you not think He will care for you? He knows your needs before you even ask. Place your hope and trust in Him. He is able. He's proved Himself over and over. By reading the scriptures and praying to the one who loves you, you can feel His care is infinite. His word is final. God loves you.

Lord, help me see You gave Your life for me.
Teach me to trust in You. Amen.

Unconditional Love

Neither height nor depth, nor anything else in all creation, will be able to separate us from the love of God that is in Christ Jesus our Lord.
ROMANS 8:39 NIV

To try to compare God's love to human love is nearly impossible. We love our families and our closest friends. But is our love unconditional? Families have divided for incidents as minor as a lack of understanding or an unexpected flare-up. Disagreements, hurt feelings, or built-up anger have caused many people to sever precious ties.

God's love, however, is unconditional. His love isn't based on our good deeds. It isn't grounded in our personal goodness or faithfulness. When we sin, He forgives. If we fall, He lifts us up and helps us go forward. He isn't easily angered, and He doesn't turn His back when we do or say something disapproving.

What would happen if we exercised God's love toward others? If we didn't take offense when someone was offensive, if we forgave when wronged, if we prayed instead of accused, if we loved even when someone failed to love us?

As Christians, nothing can separate us from God's unconditional love that is rooted in a personal relationship with Jesus. God loves you no matter what. Go and do the same.

Father, thank You for the unconditional love You show me every day. Help me to extend that love to others. Amen.

Look Up!

Your love, LORD, reaches to the heavens, your faithfulness to the skies.
PSALM 36:5 NIV

. . . .

In Bible times, people often studied the sky. Looking up at the heavens reminded them of God and His mighty wonders. A rainbow was God's sign to Noah that a flood would never again destroy the earth. God used a myriad of stars to foretell Abraham's abundant family, and a single star heralded Christ's birth.

The theme of the heavens traverses the scriptures from beginning to end. The Bible's first words say: "In the beginning God created the heavens." The psalmist David shows God's greatness in comparison to them: "the heavens declare the glory of God" (Psalm 19:1 NIV). And in the New Testament, Jesus describes the end times saying, "There will be signs in the sun, moon and stars. . . . At that time people will see the Son of Man coming in clouds with great power and glory" (Luke 21:25, Mark 13:26 NIV).

Some of God's greatest works have happened in the sky.

This immense space that we call *sky* is a reflection of God's infinite love and faithfulness. It reaches far beyond what one can see or imagine, all the way to heaven. Too often jobs, maintaining households, parenting, and other tasks keep us from looking up. So take time today. Look up at the heavens, and thank God for His endless love.

Heavenly Father, remind me to stop and appreciate Your wonderful creation. And as I look upward, fill me with Your infinite love. Amen.

What's Your Gift?

Yes, my brother, please do me this favor for the Lord's
sake. Give me this encouragement in Christ.
PHILEMON 1:20 NLT

. . . .

Encouragement comes in many forms. A standing ovation and generous applause encourage the performer. Sports teams are uplifted through the cheers of loyal fans. For the Christian, nothing compares to the encouragement we receive from one another through God's love.

The world is full of competition; consequently, words of encouragement are few. Sadly, the body of Christ often does the same, as jealousy blocks the flow of encouragement toward our brothers and sisters in Christ.

Every believer is gifted in different ways. Yet we often covet another's God-given gift. We wish we could sing or recite scriptures or teach like others. Yet God equips every believer with different talents.

Have you found yours? Often the greatest gifts are ones behind the scenes. The intercessors who pray daily for the pastors and leaders are greatly gifted with the power of the Holy Spirit to target and pray for whomever God puts on their hearts. Some possess the gift of giving—not just financially, but of themselves. Others possess God's wisdom and share a word that someone desperately needs. Where would we be without these loving, caring people?

Imprisoned, Paul wrote to Philemon asking him for a favor, indicating it would be of great encouragement to him. Similarly, God encourages us to encourage too.

Lord, help me encourage others just as You encourage me. Amen.

My Strength

I love you, LORD, my strength.
PSALM 18:1 NIV

- -

Ever feel like you want to crawl in a hole and pull the earth in around you? Most of us have felt that way at some point. Sometimes life overwhelms us, and we feel like we will drown at any moment.

At times like that, we often don't have the strength to even pray. We don't know what to say to God, and we don't have the energy to form the correct words or thoughts. That's when we need to keep it simple. "I love You, Lord" is all we need to say.

When we utter those four little words to God, we bend His ear to us. We bend His heart to us. When we whisper our love for Him, though we don't have strength to say another word, He shows up and becomes our strength. He wraps His mighty arms around us, pulls us into His lap of love and comfort, and pours His life and love into our spirits.

Truly, it is in those moments of weakness, when we have nothing else to offer God, that He is made strong in us. He longs for our love above all else. When we give it, as weak as we may feel, He becomes strength for us.

Dear Father, sometimes I feel weak, like I can't go
on. But Lord, I love You, even then. I know in my
weak moments, You are my strength. Amen.

Fellowship

*And let us consider how we may spur one another on. . .not giving
up meeting together. . .but encouraging one another.*
HEBREWS 10:24–25 NIV

. . . .

Before his conversion, Paul, then known as Saul, was a thug—a mean-spirited man who hated Christians and wanted them killed. Isn't it amazing that this same man became a great apostle who wrote thirteen books of the New Testament?

The Bible says that immediately after his conversion, Paul spent several days with Jesus' disciples. "At once" he began preaching that Jesus was the Messiah. The Bible also says that Paul became increasingly powerful, and he had followers. He traveled with other Christians, and they encouraged one another in their belief and commitment. Paul enjoyed being with other believers. When in prison, he lamented that he couldn't be with them to share encouragement. Paul understood the importance of fellowship.

Associating with other Christians is more than attending church on Sundays. It is getting to know them on a personal level and discovering what their faith has to offer in fellowship and learning. Paul sought after people whose own gifts would help build his faith. In Romans 1:11–12, he writes, "I long to see you so that I may impart to you some spiritual gift to make you strong—that is, that you and I may be mutually encouraged by each other's faith" (NIV).

Do you have friends who encourage your faith?

Dear God, thank You for sweet fellowship
with Christian friends. Amen.

35

Comfort for Comfort

For this reason Jesus had to be made like his brothers and sisters in every way so he could be their merciful and faithful high priest in service to God. Then Jesus could die in their place to take away their sins. And now he can help those who are tempted, because he himself suffered and was tempted.
HEBREWS 2:17–18 NCV

God chose to come to earth in human form to be made like us. To experience what it's like to be human. To be able to fully take our place and remove our sins. Because He was fully human while being fully God, He can help. He can comfort. The Bible says that He "comforts us in all our troubles, so that we can comfort those in any trouble with the comfort we ourselves receive from God" (2 Corinthians 1:4 NIV).

It's so encouraging to know that Jesus was just like us! Our God is not one who wants to remain as a distant high king, out of touch with the commoners. He wants a very personal relationship with each one of us. He lowered Himself to our level so that we could have personal and continuous access to Him. His glory knows no bounds, yet He desires to be our friend. Take great comfort in that.

And then when people around you are troubled, you can step in. You can wrap your arms around someone else who needs a friend because of what Jesus has done for you.

Dear Jesus, thank You for the great gift of Your
friendship. Allow me the opportunity to be a friend
and comfort to those around me in need. Amen.

Trials and Wisdom

Consider it pure joy, my brothers and sisters, whenever you face trials of many
kinds, because you know that the testing of your faith produces perseverance.
Let perseverance finish its work so that you may be mature and complete,
not lacking anything. If any of you lacks wisdom, you should ask God,
who gives generously to all without finding fault, and it will be given to you.
JAMES 1:2–5 NIV

Trials and troubles are an everyday part of living here in a fallen world. Pastor and author Max Lucado says, "Lower your expectations of earth. This isn't heaven, so don't expect it to be."

Things won't be easy and simple until we get to heaven. So how can we lift our chins and head into tomorrow without succumbing to discouragement? We remember that God is good. We trust His faithfulness. We ask for His presence and peace during each moment. We pray for wisdom and believe that the God who holds the universe in His hands is working every single trial and triumph together for our good and for His glory.

James 1:2–5 tells us that when we lack wisdom we should simply ask God for it! We don't have to face our problems alone. We don't have to worry that God will hold our past mistakes against us. Be encouraged that the Lord will give you wisdom generously without finding fault!

Lord Jesus, please give me wisdom. So many troubles
are weighing me down. Help me give You all my burdens
and increase my faith and trust in You. Amen.

Choose Love

"I give you a new command: Love each other. You must love each other as I have loved you. All people will know that you are my followers if you love each other."
<small>JOHN 13:34–35 NCV</small>

There are people in your life that you can't help but butt heads with—the ones that get under your skin, rub you the wrong way, and push your buttons at a moment's notice. They can cause an eruption of emotion within you just by entering the room—people you work with, go to church with, and, unfortunately, even those within your own family.

So, how do you keep the volcano from exploding and causing deep hurts in your relationships? Jesus gave a command to love; and because we love Him, we have the ability to live each day in His love.

The Bible says, "God's love has been poured out into our hearts through the Holy Spirit" (Romans 5:5 NIV). It's not your love but God's love that responds to those button-pushing moments. Imagine taking your irritations and dropping your emotional reaction into the sea of God's love that flows through your heart. It disappears in the flood, and then you can love out of His overflow of love for others.

Heavenly Father, remind me to take a deep breath
and choose to love no matter the circumstances.
Help me to love others as You do by living out of Your
love and responding to them as You would. Amen.

Prayer Changes Things

One day Jesus told his disciples a story to show that
they should always pray and never give up.
LUKE 18:1 NLT

Have you ever felt like you don't have enough energy to utter one more word to anyone, let alone share your feelings with the Lord? Or maybe you've been asking God for the same thing over and over again, and you feel like He either is not listening or has decided not to answer.

Jesus gives us a picture of how He wants us to pray in Luke 18. The persistent widow wears down the judge with her constant request until he finally gives in. God wants us to come to Him with everything. He has given us an open door to approach His throne with confidence at all times (Hebrews 4:16).

If an uncaring judge finally responded to the widow's constant pleas, how much more will the God who created us and loves us respond to ours? No matter what you are bringing before the Lord, don't give up! Keep talking to Him. The process will change your heart to be more like His. So when you feel all prayed out, remember that God is listening and working on your behalf.

Heavenly Father, sometimes I feel like the persistent
widow when I come to You over and over again with the
same request. I know You hear my prayer, and I trust that
You will do what is best for me. Help me not to lose heart
but to remember Your love and faithfulness. Amen.

God's Spirit is right there with us as we make decisions, as we go about our day, as we face trials, and as we enjoy His blessings.

Fully Equipped

*His divine power has given us everything we need for a godly life through
our knowledge of him who called us by his own glory and goodness.
Through these he has given us his very great and precious promises,
so that through them you may participate in the divine nature, having
escaped the corruption in the world caused by evil desires.*

2 PETER 1:3–4 NIV

As Christians, we are fully equipped to live a godly life on earth. We don't
have to live in a state of constant confusion. We don't have to stress about
what to do or how to live. God has given us everything we need to be able
to follow Him daily.

Second Corinthians 1:21–22 (NIV) tells us, "He anointed us, set his seal of
ownership on us, and put his Spirit in our hearts as a deposit, guaranteeing
what is to come." When we accept Christ as our Savior and Lord of our life,
God gives us *His Spirit*! He places *His very own Spirit* in *our* hearts! Isn't that
amazing? Take some time to fully reflect on that!

John 15:26 (NCV) calls the Holy Spirit our "Helper." We are never alone.
God's Spirit is right there with us as we make decisions, as we go about our
day, as we face trials, and as we enjoy His blessings. We have a constant
Helper everywhere we go!

Heavenly Father, I'm amazed at what You've done.
Thank You for placing Your Spirit in my heart.
Help me to listen as You lead and guide me! Amen.

Everlasting Light

In him was life, and that life was the light of all mankind.
The light shines in the darkness, and the darkness has not overcome it.

John 1:4–5 NIV

We all experience times of darkness in our lives. Depression may seep in through a crack of doubt, fear, or worry; and we spiral downward, focusing on the situation. It's not easy to lift our voices in anything but a moan and a plea for God's help. And He hears those cries; He wants to carry our burdens for us. He listens. It's we who should shift our gaze.

Focus on the fact that Jesus is the Light of the World who holds out wonderful hope for us. Set your prayer life to start with praise and adoration of the King of kings. Lift your voice in song or read out loud from the Word. The Light will eliminate the darkness every time. Keep your heart and mind set on Him as you walk through the day. Praise for every little thing; nothing is too small for God. Did you get a great parking spot? Thank Him. A raise at work? Thank Him. A terrible headache? Praise anyway. Concentrate on His goodness instead of your pain.

A grateful heart and constant praise will bring the Light into your day.

Dear Lord, how we love You. We trust in You this day to
lead us on the right path lit with Your light. Amen.

True Friendship

Rejoice with those who rejoice; mourn with those who mourn.
ROMANS 12:15 NIV

. . . .

True Christian friendship has this verse stamped all over it. Do you have a friend who truly finds joy in your successes? When you are on top of the world, this person is genuinely happy for you. When you are sad, you have seen tears come to her eyes. This is not a friendship found every day. It is rare and to be treasured.

As believers in Christ, we have this high call on our lives. Pray that you might truly celebrate with others, not secretly wishing you were the one receiving the blessing. On the other hand, know that at times sorrow and loss are so deep that a hug and an "I love you" will mean the world. Lots of words are not needed in such times. To mourn with the mourner is the greatest gift you can give. Just to show up, to extend help, to show love.

If you have such a friend, you no doubt cherish her. Make it your aim to live out Romans 12:15 in small ways this week. Stand and cheer when others are victorious. Stand close by and be ready to comfort them when they experience disappointment or loss.

Heavenly Father, help me to rejoice with those who
rejoice and to mourn with those who mourn. Give me
a sensitive heart that is focused on others. Amen.

Step by Step

*For we walk by faith [we regulate our lives and conduct
ourselves by our conviction or belief. . .with trust and holy
fervor; thus we walk] not by sight or appearance.*

2 CORINTHIANS 5:7 AMPC

The experiences and circumstances of our lives can often lead us to lose heart. The apostle Paul exhorts us to look away from this present world and rely on God by faith. Webster's dictionary defines faith as a firm belief and complete trust. Trusting, even when our faith is small, is not an easy task. However, when we understand God is a God of faith and He works in ways that faith, not feelings, can discern, we will more easily trust Him.

Toddlers learn to walk by gripping hold of furniture or a parent's hand. They release that grip and bobble, sometimes fall, but by nature they stand once again and take another step. How they are cheered on when learning to walk! Step by wobbly step.

Today, grasp hold of God's Word and feel His presence. Hold tightly and don't let your steps falter. He is beside you and will lead you. Trusting and walking with Him is a process, much like the toddler's. Remember to look up, and if you stumble, He's there to grab hold.

Dear heavenly Father, today I choose to clutch Your
hand and feel Your presence as I trudge the pathways
of my life. I trust You are by my side. Amen.

Into His Presence

Let us come before him with thanksgiving
and extol him with music and song.
PSALM 95:2 NIV

If God is everywhere, how is it possible to come *into* His presence? While it's true that God is ever-present, His children are given a special invitation to draw near to Him. Yes, He may be at the banquet, but *we* can occupy the seat of honor right next to Him.

The way we draw near to God is through a beautiful, balanced combination of reverence and excitement. While our respect for God requires a measure of solemnity, God is no fuddy-duddy. He wants us to be happy and joyful in His presence. He longs to hear a simple, sincere, excited "thank You" from His children, for all the things He's done in the past. He longs to see us sing and dance in His presence and tell Him how much we love Him.

When God feels distant, we can remember our special invitation to join Him in intimate conversation. He will welcome us into His arms when we fall before Him, give excited thanks, and sing joyful songs of love and praise.

Dear Father, thank You for inviting me into Your presence.
Sometimes I barge right in, spouting off my list of requests,
and I forget to say "thank You." I forget to tell You how
wonderful You are. Forgive me for that. Thank You,
Father, for all You've done for me. I love You. Amen.

He Makes All Things New

*Create in me a pure heart, O God, and renew a steadfast
spirit within me. Do not cast me from your presence or take
your Holy Spirit from me. Restore to me the joy of your
salvation and grant me a willing spirit, to sustain me.*

PSALM 51:10–12 NIV

King David committed adultery and had the woman's husband killed in
battle (see Psalm 51). Talk about guilt! Yet the Bible says David was a man
after God's own heart. David truly loved God, and being a king with power,
he messed up royally!

David had faith in God's goodness. He was truly repentant and expected
to be restored to God's presence. He could not stand to be separated from
God. He recognized that he must become clean again through the power
of forgiveness.

Perhaps there have been times when you felt distant from God because
of choices you made. There is no sin that is too big for God to cover or too
small to bother Him with. He is willing to forgive, and He forgets when you
ask Him. He expects you to do the same. If you don't let forgiven sin go, it
can become a tool for torture for the enemy to use against you. God sent
Jesus to the cross for you to restore you to relationship with Him.

Heavenly Father, thank You for sending Jesus to
pay for my sins. Forgive me and make me new.
Fill me with Your presence today. Amen.

Remain in His Love

"As the Father has loved me, so have I loved you. Now remain in my love. If you keep my commands, you will remain in my love, just as I have kept my Father's commands and remain in his love."

JOHN 15:9–10 NIV

• •

Remaining in Christ's love is the only way to bear fruit that will last. John 15 gives us a beautiful picture of what bearing fruit means. What kind of fruit are we talking about here? The kind of fruit that makes a difference for Christ. The fruits of the Spirit are love, joy, peace, patience, kindness, goodness, faithfulness, gentleness, and self-control (Galatians 5:22–23). These are the fruits that honor God and come from a life that is growing in Him.

The Bible says that if we remain in God's love, we will bear much fruit. So how do we remain in His love? John 15:10 tells us the answer: "If you keep my commands, you will remain in my love." We can have complete joy and bear all kinds of spiritual fruit if we follow God's Word and live a life that pleases Him.

Just as a branch that has been cut off from the vine can do nothing, we can do nothing that matters if we aren't connected to the vine.

Father, help me stay connected to You so that
I can bear the kind of fruit that matters. I know
I can do nothing good without You. Amen.

Hannah's Prayer

"The eyes of the Lord search the whole earth in order to
strengthen those whose hearts are fully committed to him."
2 Chronicles 16:9 nlt

. . . .

There are many great prayers in the Bible. There are prayers for wisdom and for unity, prayers of repentance and negotiation with God. Hannah's was an anguished prayer for a child.

Hannah was barren. She prayed before God with a broken heart and promised God that if He gave her a child, she would commit him to the Lord all the days of his life. God heard and answered her prayer. Does God always answer the prayer for a child in this way? No, He doesn't. There are women whom God loves deeply and unconditionally who will not bear a child in this life. But in this case, God granted Hannah a male child whom she named Samuel. She only had Samuel for a short time before she took him to Eli, the priest. Samuel was not an ordinary child. He heard the voice of God at a very young age. He grew up to become a judge and prophet that could not be matched in all of Israel's history.

God is looking for ordinary men and women whose prayers reflect hearts completely committed to Him. He found such commitment in Hannah, and He answered her prayer.

Father, may my prayers reflect a deep commitment
to You, and may all that I ask for be for Your
kingdom and not for my own glory. Amen.

Ready for Change

*"If my people, who are called by my name, will humble themselves and
pray and seek my face and turn from their wicked ways, then I will hear
from heaven, and I will forgive their sin and will heal their land."*

2 CHRONICLES 7:14 NIV

How we yearn for the "good old days." Many of us remember our childhood
years with nostalgia about a kinder, gentler time. We think that things were
much better then. King Solomon might have thought the same thing when
this verse was given to him at the dedication of the temple. The verse is a
call for revival.

Revival doesn't have to be a corporate event. Sometimes, it needs to be
personal. The statement is conditional: if we will meet the requirements on
our end, we can be sure that God will move on His end.

Sovereign God, I come to You wanting revival in my life.
I humble myself before You, understanding that I cannot
do anything without You. Please rekindle my desire for
You and hear my pledge to erase anything from my life
that does not please You. I know that You will hear me;
help me and heal me as You have promised. Amen!

Stay Teachable

When Apollos wanted to go to Achaia, the brothers and sisters
encouraged him and wrote to the disciples there to welcome him.
ACTS 18:27 NIV

. . . .

Apollos was a powerhouse for the Lord. The scriptures describe him as "a learned man, with a thorough knowledge of the Scriptures. . . . He spoke with great fervor and taught about Jesus accurately" (Acts 18:24–25 NIV).

So it's interesting that even with those credentials, Priscilla and Aquila, having heard him, invited him to their house for additional teaching. Afterward, Apollos desired to preach in Achaia, and the couple encouraged him to do so. They immediately contacted the disciples there to welcome him. The result? Apollos refuted the Jews in public debate, proving that Jesus was the Messiah while helping the apostles at the same time (Acts 18:27–28).

We all have room for spiritual growth and godly knowledge no matter how long we have known the Lord. The Bible urges us to encourage one another. What would happen to advance the kingdom if all believers, despite their position or spiritual seniority, exercised the humility of Apollos? Though scholarly, he accepted more instruction from other believers who, in turn, encouraged his ministry. Jealousy, pride, or one-upmanship didn't exist.

We are to encourage one another, just as God encourages us.

Lord, keep me teachable so that I can become more effective
for You to encourage others in their ministries. Amen.

Stop, Breathe, Pray. . . and Repeat

Do not be anxious about anything, but in every situation, by prayer and petition, with thanksgiving, present your requests to God. And the peace of God, which transcends all understanding, will guard your hearts and your minds in Christ Jesus.
PHILIPPIANS 4:6–7 NIV

Being a woman in these times is challenging. Many of us are working demanding jobs, managing our homes and crazy schedules, and taking care of children or aging parents. Often, we feel we don't have enough time to get everything done, let alone take care of ourselves properly. All of this creates stress and anxiety, which just makes many of these situations worse.

What can you do when it seems the world is falling down around your feet? Stop. Take a deep breath and settle your mind on Jesus. Give Him the situation, the harried thoughts, the worries. God says that we can take anything to Him in prayer! He will provide whatever we need, even the peace that will get us through the most difficult circumstances.

Father God, we are thankful that we can take any worried thought or situation to You in prayer. You tell us that You will provide for us and will even give us Your peace! Help us to trust You in this, Lord, to lay the situation at Your feet and leave it there. Fill our minds and hearts with Your peace and remind us of how much You love us. Amen!

Unshakable Love

*"For even if the mountains walk away and the hills fall to pieces,
my love won't walk away from you, my covenant commitment of peace
won't fall apart." The GOD who has compassion on you says so.*
ISAIAH 54:10 MSG

As modern women, anxiety seems to stalk us. Our newsfeeds mention uprisings, terrorist attacks, market fluctuations, and hurricanes. Fear is a very common reaction to the world's instability, and it can easily cloud our mind and turn us into quaking, terrified children. The question is, do we want to dissolve into frightened, anxious women who rarely step outside our comfort zones, or do we desire to be bold, unashamed, fearless women of the Most High King?

God doesn't want us to cower beneath the weight of uncertainty. Instead, through the scriptures, other believers, and the indwelling Holy Spirit, He encourages us to be bold, passionate, and faithful. But how do we bridge the gap between our emotions and His desires for us?

The answer: love. We must rest in God's wild, unbending love for us. He promises in Isaiah that no matter what happens, He will never remove Himself from us. When we believe Him wholeheartedly and rest in His love, we will be filled with fear-busting peace and adventurous faith. That faith allows us to dream big dreams and conquer the worries that keep us chained.

Lord, thank You for Your love, which never leaves me.
Help me to rest in Your love above all else. Amen.

GOD DOESN'T
WANT US TO COWER
BENEATH THE WEIGHT
OF UNCERTAINTY.
INSTEAD. . .
HE ENCOURAGES US TO
be bold, passionate,
and faithful.

Renew Your Strength

But those who wait for the Lord [who expect, look for, and hope in Him]
shall change and renew their strength and power; they shall lift their wings
and mount up [close to God] as eagles [mount up to the sun]; they shall
run and not be weary, they shall walk and not faint or become tired.
ISAIAH 40:31 AMPC

Andrew Murray was a South African writer, teacher, and Christian pastor in the late 1800s who captured the heart of prayer with these words about Jesus: "While others still slept, He went away to pray and to renew His strength in communion with His Father. He had need of this, otherwise He would not have been ready for the new day. The holy work of delivering souls demands constant renewal through fellowship with God."

Each day, you give a part of yourself to that day—spiritually, emotionally, physically, financially, and socially. Within each of those areas of life, you need to refuel. Spiritually, the only way to recharge is a renewal that comes from God. Waiting for a fresh outpouring of His life-giving Spirit brings a renewed perspective on all the other areas of your life. Give your best each day by drawing on the strength of your heavenly Father and spending time with Him.

Heavenly Father, Your Word and prayer are strength to
my soul. Renew me and pour Your life into me. Fill me with
Your power and give me courage for a new day. Amen.

Don't Worry!

Don't worry about anything; instead, pray about everything.
Tell God what you need, and thank him for all he has done. Then you will
experience God's peace, which exceeds anything we can understand.
His peace will guard your hearts and minds as you live in Christ Jesus.

PHILIPPIANS 4:6–7 NLT

The Bible tells us plainly not to worry. But that can be difficult when the economy is poor, bills need to be paid, health issues arise, and families face crisis after crisis. Jesus helps us make sense of this in Luke 12:25 (NIV): "Who of you by worrying can add a single hour to your life?" The answer is obvious. It can't be done. So why waste precious time and energy worrying when it will change nothing?

When you start to worry, pray instead. Tell God how you feel and what you need. Tell Him that you're struggling with worry and ask Him to take your fears away. He replies to your heartfelt plea gently in Luke 12:32 (NIV): "Do not be afraid, little flock, for your Father has been pleased to give you the kingdom."

How comforting, those words from the mouth of Jesus! Don't be afraid! Don't worry! You've got the kingdom of God to look forward to for all eternity. No need to worry about the rest.

Dear Jesus, thank You for Your promise of
eternal life! Give me peace that exceeds my
understanding when I start to worry. Amen.

The Ultimate Act of Love

*Bring joy to your servant, Lord, for I put my trust in you. You, Lord,
are forgiving and good, abounding in love to all who call to you.*
PSALM 86:4–5 NIV

The modern theologian Lewis Smedes once said, "You will know that forgiveness has begun when you recall those who hurt you and feel the power to wish them well." It seems the most unnatural thing in the world for us to forgive someone who has hurt us deeply, let alone hoping good things will happen for them. However, that is really the only loving thing to do.

Forgiveness doesn't require that the person who did the hurting apologize or acknowledge what they've done. It's not about making the score even. It doesn't even require forgetting about the incident. But it is about admitting that the one who hurt us is human, just like we are. We surrender our right for revenge and, like God, let go and give the wrongdoer mercy, therefore blessing them.

Gracious and loving Father, thank You that You love me and have forgiven me of my sins. May I be more like You in forgiving others. Although I may not be able to forgive as easily as You do, please encourage me to take those small steps. In forgiving others, Father, I am that much closer to being like You. Amen.

No Harm

Love does no harm to a neighbor. Therefore love is the fulfillment of the law.
ROMANS 13:10 NIV

. . . .

Love does no harm. Ever. That is a powerful statement.

If love does no wrong to a neighbor, that means love never utters cruel words. Love never gossips. Love is never violent, never impatient, never easily angered. And love certainly never plans out mean, vicious actions.

Love does only good to the people around us. Only good.

Unfortunately, none of us loves perfectly—yet. And we won't love perfectly until we're made perfect by our Creator, when we stand before Him. Until then, we will mess up. We will act in unloving ways sometimes.

The key is to make love a habit and admit when we've not acted in love. When we catch ourselves thinking unkind thoughts, we need to get our thoughts in line, for unkind thoughts lead to unkind actions. When we let our tongues slip and we say cruel things, we should apologize. And we need to continually examine our hearts and our motives, to see if we're being ruled by love.

Love always builds up, always points people to the source of love—God. And since God's love for each and every one of His children is perfect and complete, we must work to deliver that kind of love as well.

Dear Father, forgive me for the times I have been
cruel or thoughtless and have not acted in love.
Help me to make love a way of everyday life. Amen.

The Lord Is Close

Everything the LORD does is right. He is loyal to all he has made.
The LORD is close to everyone who prays to him, to all who truly pray to him.
PSALM 145:17–18 NCV

Do you ever feel like you go to God in prayer with the same things over and over again? Is your prayer life in need of a little lift? The Psalms are full of prayers and truth. To find a road map for prayers and promises, look to the Psalms.

The authors of the Psalms knew the truth of this scripture—that the Lord is close to those who pray to Him. They expressed their honest emotions to God—their joy, their fears, their praise. They understood that God loved them and wanted to have a personal relationship with them—just like He does with us.

If you're struggling with how to pray to God or what to pray about, use the Psalms as your guide. Pray through a psalm every day. Add your own personal thoughts and feelings as you pray. Pretty soon, you'll realize that you have begun a personal friendship with the Creator of the universe.

How amazing that You, Lord, Creator of heaven and
earth, want to know me intimately! Thank You for loving
me and showing Yourself to me through Your Word
and Your creation. Thank You for being close to me
so that I can know You and live for You. Amen.

Providing It All

For God so greatly loved and dearly prized the world that He [even] gave up His only begotten (unique) Son, so that whoever believes in (trusts in, clings to, relies on) Him shall not perish (come to destruction, be lost) but have eternal (everlasting) life.

JOHN 3:16 AMPC

Beginning with Adam, God provided for His loved ones: a ram for Abraham to spare his son, manna for the wandering Jewish people. The Bible resonates with the provisions of a mighty God. And the Word says our God is the same today as He was then. So we know He will provide for our needs. True love is reflected in His care for us every day.

His provision is not just for our material needs, but more importantly He extends us unmerited favor, grace, when we least deserve it. He provides us with an all-encompassing love once we accept it. And He seals His promises with the gift of the Holy Spirit, making us heirs to the throne. When we realize the depth of care we've received from our heavenly Father, it is breathtaking.

Always a step ahead, He made provision before any need existed. God gave us His all, His best, when He gave us His Son. He provided it all. We serve a glorious and mighty God.

Lord, Your encompassing love amazes me. Thank You for all
You have done and will continue to do in my life. Amen.

Building Friendships

A friend loves at all times, and a brother is born for a time of adversity.
PROVERBS 17:17 NIV

Today's world isn't designed for friendship. It's too fast paced, with too many demands and too much stress. Oh, we're connected to everyone, all the time, through text messaging and cell phones and social media. But none of these is a true replacement for face-to-face time. We're so distracted with everything at once, we find it hard to focus on one thing, one person at a time.

But friendship demands one-on-one, face-to-face time. And although most of us don't feel we have a lot of time to give, we must! We simply must make friendship, and building real flesh-and-blood relationships, a priority.

God created us for relationships. And although a well-timed email or text message may lift us up at times, there's simply no replacement for a real, live hug. There's no substitute for a friend sitting beside you in the hospital, holding your hand. And we won't have those things unless we're willing to put aside our high-tech gadgets and invest time in the people around us.

Today, let's make it a point to set down our phones. Let's step away from our computers for a while and have a real conversation with someone. That person may just turn out to be a true friend.

Dear Father, teach me to be a true friend. Help me to make friendship a priority and invest in the people around me. Amen.

The Way Out

No temptation has overtaken you except what is common to mankind. And God is faithful; he will not let you be tempted beyond what you can bear. But when you are tempted, he will also provide a way out so that you can endure it.

1 CORINTHIANS 10:13 NIV

- -

Everyone faces temptation. Scripture says that no one escapes it, and all become its victims (Romans 3:23). But don't be discouraged. God provides a way out.

Believers learn to endure and stand up to temptation by God's grace. When they rely on the power that comes from the Holy Spirit, then God provides them with strength to resist. Jesus said that this willpower comes by watchfulness and prayer. "Watch and pray so that you will not fall into temptation. The spirit is willing, but the flesh is weak" (Matthew 26:41 NIV).

As hard as people try, temptation sometimes wins. God has a plan for that too. He sent His Son, Jesus, into the world to take the punishment for the sins of everyone who believes in Him. Not only did Jesus suffer the consequences of sin but also through His sacrifice He provided God with a way to forgive sinfulness and to promise believers eternal life.

Watch and pray today that you don't fall into temptation, but if you do, then remember this: sin might win in the moment, but God's grace and forgiveness are forever.

Dear Lord, lead me not into temptation but deliver
me from evil today and always. Amen.

Just in Time

Let us then fearlessly and confidently and boldly draw near to the throne of grace (the throne of God's unmerited favor to us sinners), that we may receive mercy [for our failures] and find grace to help in good time for every need [appropriate help and well-timed help, coming just when we need it].
HEBREWS 4:16 AMPC

As believers, our lives become exciting when we wait on God to direct our paths, because He knows what is best for us at any given moment. His plans and agenda are never wrong. We just need to practice living on His schedule and spending time in prayer. But that's easier said than done! Often we are chomping at the bit, and it's hard to wait.

Once we fully realize He knows best and turn our lives over to the Spirit for direction, we can allow God to be in charge of our calendar; His timing is what is paramount.

When chomping at the bit for a job offer or for a proposal, His timing might seem slow. "Hurry up, God!" we groan. But when we learn to patiently wait on His promises, we will see the plans He has for us are more than we dared hope—or dream. God promises to answer us; and it never fails to be just in time.

Lord, I want Your perfect will in my life.
Help me learn to wait on You. Amen.

Lead Us, Lord

I know, GOD, that mere mortals can't run their own lives, that men and women don't have what it takes to take charge of life. So correct us, GOD, as you see best.
JEREMIAH 10:23–24 MSG

So many changes would happen in our lives if we lived Jeremiah's words—if we really believed God was in control. We would be able to release our worries and problems in a prayer of thanksgiving and then wait. And that's the difficulty that trips us up. In our frenzied world, we feel we need immediate answers, and we rush to solve situations our own way. Sometimes that works; however, often we become enmeshed in less than desirable circumstances.

The last line of the scripture entreats God to correct us, and that's certainly not a desirous thought. Not many hope to be straightened out. But when we yield our lives to Him and trust Him implicitly, understanding full well that our Creator God wants the best for us, then our prayers of thanksgiving and trust fall more easily from our mouths. Adoration and praise should fall from our lips before our requests.

A prayer of total surrender gives glory to God the Father and pleases Him. It allows Him to work in our lives in ways we often don't understand.

Lord, I bless You and give You my heartfelt praise.
Thank You for all You do to work on my behalf. Amen.

Plunge
INTO THE RIVER OF
[GOD'S] LOVE
AND FEEL HIM
CARRY YOU
ON ITS
current.

Love's Current

The grace of our Lord was poured out on me abundantly,
along with the faith and love that are in Christ Jesus.
1 TIMOTHY 1:14 NIV

Giving a gift to a loved one often gives us great pleasure. We shop in anticipation of the recipient's excitement at our purchases. When we love that person, our joy can be even greater. So it is with God's love for us. He gave us His Son, a pure and perfect gift, because He loves us in vast measure.

No matter what our attitude may be toward God, we can never forget His precious gift of Jesus Christ. Even if we reflect despair or anger, He loves us. The Bible tells us that God gives us grace and love abundantly, which means bountifully, plenteously, generously. How can we miss God's love when He is so gracious?

The famous theologian Charles Spurgeon put it this way: "Our God never ceases to shine upon his children with beams of love. Like a river, his lovingkindness is always flowing, with a fullness inexhaustible as his own nature."

This day, rise with the expectation of God's great grace and love. Let your life reflect that love and feel His pleasure. Plunge into the river of His love and feel Him carry you on its current. Relax in His arms in the knowledge that He cares for you.

Lord, carry me along in the current of Your love's
stream. I love You extravagantly. Amen.

Praying for Our Loved Ones

*"Therefore I tell you, whatever you ask for in prayer,
believe that you have received it, and it will be yours."*

MARK 11:24 NIV

One of the best things we can do for our friends and family members is pray for them. And while there isn't one single formula for prayer in the Bible, we can take cues from the prayers of people in the Bible.

Are we like the Pharisees as we talk to our heavenly Father, asking Him to change others—but neglecting to ask Him to change us? Do we take responsibility for the hurts we have caused, like David did in the Psalms? Do we pray with thanksgiving, like Mary did after Gabriel came to her?

Do we ask God in faith, believing—as Hannah did—that He can do anything? Or do we pray in hesitation, lacking conviction? We could also learn a lot from the prayers of Paul in his letters to the churches he ministered to. Many of his prayers can be prayed verbatim for those we love.

We also find help and hope when we sit in silence, listening in prayer. God, through His Holy Spirit, can give us wisdom, endurance, and insight we would never come up with on our own.

Though we can't always see it, He is at work. . .in our loved ones' hearts—and in ours.

Lord, thank You for Your concern for those I love.
I know You love them even more than I do. Amen.

Pray for Christian Households

When she speaks, her words are wise, and she gives instructions with kindness.

PROVERBS 31:26 NLT

. . . .

Is there a Christian woman whom you admire, someone who has helped you grow in your faith? In Paul's second letter to Timothy, he mentioned two special women in Timothy's life: "I am reminded of your sincere faith, which first lived in your grandmother Lois and in your mother Eunice and, I am persuaded, now lives in you also" (2 Timothy 1:5 NIV). How precious it is in God's sight when children are raised in households where He is the foundation and family is the priority.

In Christian households, children learn about God's love and faithfulness. Discipline is administered out of loving-kindness, not anger, and love is taught through the parents' example. It is a home in which Christlike wisdom is passed from generation to generation.

In Timothy's household, he learned from his mother and grandmother's faith, and according to Paul, those seeds of faith grew in young Timothy and led him to become a servant of the Lord.

Whether you are married or single, have children or not, you can plant seeds of faith through your own Christian example and prayer. Pray for all children that they will grow up in godly homes, and pray for women everywhere that they will raise their children in Christian households and remain always faithful to God.

Heavenly Father, shine Your light through me today
that I might be an example to others. Amen.

Keep Talking

The LORD is near to all who call on him, to all who call on him in truth.
PSALM 145:18 NIV

God is everywhere, all the time. In a sense, He's near to everyone, since there's no place we can hide from His presence. But the word *near* in this verse refers to a sense of spiritual, emotional closeness. I might be in the same room with a hundred strangers, but I wouldn't consider myself *close* to any of them. But if you ask me about my best friend who lives across the country, I'd tell you we're very close.

When we call on God, no matter our circumstances, we become close to Him. He sees our hearts, He has compassion on us, and He longs to pull us into His arms and hold us there. When we call on Him, when we spend time talking to Him and telling Him what's on our minds, we strengthen our relationship with Him.

We get *close* to Him.

When we feel far from God, sometimes the last thing we want to do is talk to Him. But it is through honest, heartfelt conversation, however one-sided it may seem to us, that we draw into God's presence. When we feel far from God, we need to keep talking. He's there.

Dear Father, thank You for Your promise to listen to me.
I love You, I need You, and I want to be close to You. Amen.

Biblical Encouragement for Women

Don't be concerned about the outward beauty of fancy hairstyles, expensive jewelry, or beautiful clothes. You should clothe yourselves instead with the beauty that comes from within, the unfading beauty of a gentle and quiet spirit, which is so precious to God.

1 PETER 3:3–4 NLT

The world encourages women to dress provocatively, to invest in expensive products and styles, all to make them "better." This is not how God judges a woman's heart. God is concerned with what is on the inside. He listens to how you respond to others and watches the facial expressions you choose to exhibit. He sees your heart. Certainly it is fun to buy a new outfit or spend some time and effort accessorizing. There is nothing wrong with this in and of itself. Where the trouble comes is when the world's messages drown out God's call on your life. The Lord desires that you clothe yourself with a gentle and quiet spirit. He declares this as unfading beauty, the inner beauty of the heart. Focus on this and no one will even notice whether your jewelry shines. Your face will be radiant with the joy of the Lord and your heart will overflow with grace and peace.

Lord, grant me a quiet and gentle spirit.
I ask this in Jesus' name. Amen.

Who God Hears

The L ORD is far from the wicked, but he hears the prayers of the righteous.
PROVERBS 15:29 NLT

One of the countless, wonderful things about God is that He's a gentleman. As powerful as He is, He rarely pushes in where He's not wanted, except in cases where justice demands it.

God remains far from the wicked, for the wicked push Him away. They don't want Him around. They make choices against the Almighty and disregard His ways. Then, when they land themselves in trouble with no way out, help is nowhere to be found. They choose to exclude the One who could help them. In the end, they have no one.

But when the righteous call His name, He hears. Though none of us is righteous on our own, we can claim righteousness through Jesus Christ. He alone is righteous, and He covers us like a cloak. When we call on God, He sees the righteousness that covers us through Christ and recognizes us as His children. He leans over and listens carefully to our words, because we belong to Him. He loves us.

Next time it seems like God isn't listening, perhaps we should examine our hearts. Have we pushed God away? Have we accepted the price His Son, Jesus Christ, paid on our behalf? If not, we can't claim righteousness. If we have, we can trust that He's never far away. He hears us.

Dear Father, thank You for making me righteous
through Your Son, Jesus. Amen.

Your Heart's Desire

Trust in the LORD and do good. Then you will live safely in the land and prosper. Take delight in the LORD, and he will give you your heart's desires. Commit everything you do to the LORD. Trust him, and he will help you.

PSALM 37:3–5 NLT

It's easy to look at this verse and think, "Hey, if I just delight in the Lord, He'll give me everything I want!" But when we really start to delight in the Lord, God changes our hearts so completely that all we ever want is what *He* wants. When you commit everything you do to the Lord, you will begin to see how your desires line up with God's desires.

What does this look like in everyday life? Start your morning with thankfulness. Ask God to bless your day and to provide opportunities to be a blessing to those you encounter. Interact with God about each issue and problem you face. Thank Him for big and little blessings that come your way. Seek His will and guidance when you make plans. Pray for loved ones who don't know Christ. Intercede for friends and neighbors who need divine help. Be on the lookout for new ways to delight yourself in the Lord.

Lord, I commit my whole heart to You—and all of my plans and ideas. I want Your will in my life. Thank You for Your blessings and Your great love for me. Show me how to delight in You, Lord. I love You. Amen.

No Greater Love

For God so loved the world that he gave his one and only Son, that whoever believes in him shall not perish but have eternal life. For God did not send his Son into the world to condemn the world, but to save the world through him.

JOHN 3:16–17 NIV

. . . .

Probably the most memorized passage of scripture, John 3:16 is the gospel in one sentence. We memorize it at an early age so our ears become accustomed to hearing it. But have you allowed it to completely change your life?

God didn't send Jesus to condemn us! He came to save us by giving up His life for ours. John 15:13 (NLT) says "there is no greater love than to lay down one's life for one's friends." That is the very foundation of Christianity. As C. S. Lewis said, "Christianity, if false, is of no importance, and if true, of infinite importance. The only thing it cannot be is moderately important."

The next time you hear a child recite John 3:16 or listen as this verse is being read aloud, allow the words to truly seep into your soul once again. Thank God for His amazing gift of life and His unfailing love for us.

Heavenly Father, thank You for the cross and its infinite importance in my life. Thank You for making a way for me to know You and live eternally with You. I give my life fully to You. Teach me how to live for You. Amen.

Second Chances

"I, even I, am he who blots out your transgressions,
for my own sake, and remembers your sins no more."
Isaiah 43:25 NIV

How many of us have hung our heads low, knowing we really messed up? Wishing we could redo that homework assignment, take back the unkind words that leaped from our mouths without thinking, or even pull back that email message right after we clicked Send. We've all done something we wished we could undo. Often, we think we have failed not only ourselves but also God.

Actually, the Bible is full of people that God used despite their errors. Moses had an anger problem. David was lustful. Jacob was deceptive. The wonderful thing about our faith is that we serve a God of second chances. Not only is He willing, but He also wants us to confess our sins so He can forgive us. Sing praises for the wonderful blessing of starting over!

Gracious and heavenly Father, we are grateful that we serve a God of second chances. In fact, You give us more than two chances, and You don't keep score. We are all prodigals, and we need to feel Your love and forgiveness. Thank You for loving me enough to not give up on me. You are still with me! Amen.

Good Gifts

"If you, then, though you are evil, know how to give good
gifts to your children, how much more will your Father
in heaven give good gifts to those who ask him!"
MATTHEW 7:11 NIV

It's a natural, God-bred instinct to care for our children. Even parents who seem to have little parental aptitude usually try to provide the basics. Yet where parents sometimes fall short, God never will.

God loves us, and He delights in caring for us. When our own children are tired or hungry or hurt, we don't want them running to some stranger for comfort. We want them to run to us, snuggle into our arms, and trust us to care for them. God is no different.

Sometimes, though, our children ask us for things we know might hurt them. A two-year-old boy might seem fascinated by the sharp knife Mommy is using to fix dinner, but she won't give it to him, and he may throw a tantrum. He won't understand that it's out of love his mother withholds the knife.

We become distracted and enamored with shiny things too. Often we see something that seems exciting and good, and we want it for ourselves. We get frustrated when God won't give it to us. But we can always trust God's heart. We can know that even when He withholds things we think will bring us happiness, He does it out of love.

Dear Father, thank You for supplying all my
needs and many of my wants. Amen.

Have You Thanked Someone Today?

They have been a wonderful encouragement to me, as they have been to you. You must show your appreciation to all who serve so well.

1 CORINTHIANS 16:18 NLT

Have you thanked your pastor, friends, or family who have encouraged or helped you just when you needed it?

Paul wrote to the Corinthian church, explaining how Stephanas and his family were the first converts in Achaia and how they devoted themselves to serve others. He reminded them that when Stephanas, Fortunatus, and Achaicus arrived in Corinth they supplied whatever needs the people had and they "refreshed my spirit and yours" (NIV).

When true believers serve, they serve from the heart, not an inward desire for outward praise. This is what Stephanas did, yet Paul still prompted the church to show appreciation for God's servant and what he did for them.

Do you ever feel taken advantage of? Do you labor and receive little to no recognition? As God's servants, we work because we love Christ; yet an occasional display of appreciation is always. . .well, appreciated. That's what Paul communicated. "Hey guys, let's encourage our brothers through showing our appreciation to them for all they did for us!"

Paul's suggestion holds true today. Thank someone who has refreshed your spirit. It will encourage them and you to keep persevering on life's pathway.

Lord, encourage me to show my appreciation to those who
have touched my life with Your love and grace. Amen.

Love Like Jesus

"Love your enemies, do good to them, and lend to them without expecting to get anything back. Then your reward will be great."
LUKE 6:35 NIV

. . . .

These words, spoken by Jesus, are some of the hardest words we have to consider. Love our enemies? Really?

The thought of loving those who do us harm just doesn't sit right. The thought of giving kindness in return for malicious intent makes no sense and causes our stomachs to knot up, our shoulders to tighten. Love our enemies? Please, God, no.

Isn't it enough to avoid our enemies and do them no harm?

Sometimes. Maybe. But most of the time, God calls us to a love so brave, so intense that it defies logic and turns the world on its side. He calls us to love like He loves.

That means we must show patience where others have been short. We must show kindness where others have been cruel. We must look for ways to bless, when others have cursed.

Something about that just doesn't feel right to our human hearts.

But God promises great rewards for those who do this. Oh, the rewards may not be immediate. But when God promises great rewards, we can know without doubt that any present struggle will be repaid with goodness and blessing, many times over.

Dear Father, help me to love those who hate me,
bless those who curse me, and show kindness to those who
have been cruel. Help me to love like You love. Amen.

76

"*Love your enemies.*"

LUKE 6:35 NIV

Pray for Others

I urge, then, first of all, that petitions, prayers,
intercession and thanksgiving be made for all people.
1 TIMOTHY 2:1 NIV

After Moses received the Ten Commandments from God on Mount Sinai, he called the Israelites together and said to them, "At the mountain the LORD spoke to you face to face from the heart of the fire. I stood as an intermediary between you and the LORD, for you were afraid of the fire and did not want to approach the mountain" (Deuteronomy 5:4–5 NLT). Moses often was the go-between between God and His people. He interceded on their behalf.

Intercessory prayer is a divine act of love and service. It requires persistence, patience, and faith in God. Christians should intercede for family and friends, their country, government leaders, their pastors, the church, the poor, the sick, the community in which they live, their enemies, and especially for those who are not saved. Wherever there is a need, Christians should pray.

The Bible holds many examples of intercessory prayer. Look for them as you read the scriptures. Discover how God's people prayed and the great changes those prayers made.

Intercessory prayer is just as important today as it was in Moses' time. It draws believers nearer to God and provides them with a powerful way to help others. Whom will you pray for today?

Heavenly Father, guide me as I pray for others. Help me to
pray for them faithfully, patiently, and persistently. Amen.

O the Deep, Deep Love of Jesus

I pray that out of his glorious riches he may strengthen you with power through his Spirit in your inner being, so that Christ may dwell in your hearts through faith. And I pray that you, being rooted and established in love, may have power, together with all the Lord's holy people, to grasp how wide and long and high and deep is the love of Christ.

Ephesians 3:16–18 NIV

The apostle Paul encouraged the people in Ephesus with his words to try to explain how far-reaching God's love was. Immeasurable. Unfathomable.

In the late 1800s, the lyricist Samuel Trevor Francis entertained the idea of ending his own life. In the midst of despair, he felt God reach out to him, and he wrote a stirring hymn echoing Paul's words. "O the deep, deep love of Jesus, vast, unmeasured, boundless, free! Rolling as a mighty ocean in its fullness over me! Underneath me, all around me, is the current of Thy love, leading onward, leading homeward to Thy glorious rest above!"

What an amazing picture. That He should care for us in such a way is almost incomprehensible. Despite our shortcomings, our sin, He loves us. It takes a measure of faith to believe in His love. When we feel a nagging thought of unworthiness, of being unlovable, trust in the Word and sing a new song. For His love is deep and wide.

Lord, thank You for loving me, even when I'm unlovable. Amen.

Jungle of Life

God's word is alive and working and is sharper than a double-edged sword.
It cuts all the way into us, where the soul and the spirit are joined, to the center
of our joints and bones. And it judges the thoughts and feelings in our hearts.
HEBREWS 4:12 NCV

Since the time Adam and Eve disobeyed God, the consequences of sin have often stood between us and God's best for our lives. Choosing a life of faith can feel like we are lost in a jungle, tangled in the underbrush. But God has given us a powerful tool that will cut through the debris of life in a fallen world—His Word.

When you take the Bible and live according to His plans, obeying Him, God's Word cuts like a machete through the entanglements of life. When you choose to use the sword of truth, it clears a path and can free you from the weights of the world that try to entrap and ensnare you.

No matter what the challenges of life are saying to you today, take His Word and speak His plans into your life. Choose His words of encouragement and peace instead of the negative things the circumstances are telling you.

God, I want to live in Your truth. I want to believe what You say about me in the Bible. Help me to speak Your words today instead of letting the problem speak to me. Help me believe. Amen.

Loving Fully

*Jesus replied: "'Love the Lord your God with all your heart
and with all your soul and with all your mind.'"*
MATTHEW 22:37 NIV

When Jesus commanded His followers to love God with all their hearts, souls, and minds, He meant that loving God fully means putting aside everything that gets in the way of a relationship with Him. Everything. That's no small order in a world filled with distractions.

So how can we set aside everything to fully love God? The answer is to shift our focus from serving ourselves to serving Him. Love requires action, and the Holy Spirit gives us power to glorify God with everything we do. Praising Him for His gifts is one way to love Him. Doing selfless acts of service for others in order to honor Him is another way. So is loving others as He loves us. Studying the Bible and being intimate with God in prayer is the ultimate act of love toward Him. When we center our lives on passionately pursuing God, we learn to love Him fully.

Loving God with heart, soul, and mind takes practice. It means thinking of Him moment by moment and working to glorify Him through every thought and action. Is it possible to love God more than we love anyone or anything else? We can try. Even though none of us will do it perfectly, trying every day is an act of love.

Dear God, I love You. Help me to love You
more through everything I do. Amen.

Difficult People

"You have heard that it was said, 'Love your neighbor and hate your enemy.' But I tell you, love your enemies and pray for those who persecute you, that you may be children of your Father in heaven."
MATTHEW 5:43–45 NIV

It's easy to thank God for the people we love, who bring joy and peace and laughter and all sorts of other good things to our lives. We thank God for our husbands, our children, our extended families, and our friends.

But what about those people we don't like? What about the people who are all-stress-and-no-bless? Are we supposed to thank God for the people who put knots in our stomachs, who make us cry, or who leave us fist-clenching, smoke-breathing angry? We know we're supposed to pray for our enemies, but do we really need to thank God for them?

Well, yes. God wants us to love our enemies, and it only stands to reason that we'd thank God for the people we love. It is through the difficult people in our lives that we grow and stretch, for they often test our faith in ways the easier relationships can't. Even though we may not see a lot of good in some people, God looks at every person and sees someone He loved enough to die for. And apart from Christ, we can be difficult people too.

Dear Father, thank You for the easy, happy relationships in my life. And thank You for the difficult people too, for they stretch me and push me toward You. Help me to love the way You do. Amen.

The Power of Prayer

*Confess your sins to each other and pray for each other so that
you may be healed. The earnest prayer of a righteous person
has great power and produces wonderful results.*

JAMES 5:16 NLT

There is power in prayer. Do you question this at times? There are many times in scripture when the fervent prayer of a believer actually changes God's mind! In James we read that the earnest prayer of a righteous person has great power and produces great results. You may be thinking that you are not righteous. Have you given your heart to Jesus? If you have accepted Him as your Savior, you have taken on the *righteousness* of Christ. Certainly you are not perfect. In your humanity, you still sin and fall short. But God sees you through a Jesus lens! And so, your prayers reach the ears of your heavenly Father.

Pray often. Pray earnestly. Pray without ceasing. Pray about everything. Prayer changes things. Look at Jesus' example of prayer during His time on earth. He went away to quiet places such as gardens to pray. He prayed in solitude. He prayed with all His heart. If anyone was busy, it was the Messiah! But Jesus always made time to pray. We ought to follow His example. Prayer changes things.

Lord, help me to believe in the power of prayer
and to make time for it daily. Amen.

Online Encouragement

*And now, dear brothers and sisters, one final thing. Fix your thoughts
on what is true, and honorable, and right, and pure, and lovely, and
admirable. Think about things that are excellent and worthy of praise.*

<small>PHILIPPIANS 4:8 NLT</small>

Negative and impure thoughts cross our minds daily. Social media and TV
don't help either. Even Christian friends jump on the bandwagon and post
thoughts and ideas online that make us cringe.

Instead of running away from connecting with people online because
you've had enough, make it your goal to be a light in what can be a very dark,
negative atmosphere. Encourage good and right thinking. Comment, post,
and share God's love with your friends as much as possible.

For the next thirty days, why not plan to post, text, or write at least one
encouraging comment every day? Post encouraging scripture; text a friend
a note to make her smile; highlight your favorite quote; share sweet stories
about your husband and kids on your feed.

Before you grumble or complain about something online, stop and fix
your thoughts on what is true, right, and pure. Then see if your comment
is still valid.

Father, help me not to run from online interaction but to
see it as a mission field. Help me be an encouragement
to everyone I communicate with online. Amen.

The End of Your Rope

Do not be far from me, for trouble is near and there is no one to help.
PSALM 22:11 NIV

. . . .

You can feel the desperation in David's prayer as you read Psalm 22. He feels utterly rejected and alone as he cries out to God.

Have you been there? Have you ever felt so alone and helpless that you are sure no one is there for you? Jesus meets us in those dark places of hopelessness. He calls to us and says, "Don't be troubled or afraid" (John 14:27 NLT). "Never will I leave you; never will I forsake you" (Hebrews 13:5 NIV). You are never alone.

The late youth evangelist Dave Busby said, "The end of your rope is God's permanent address." Jesus reaches down and wraps you in His loving arms when you call to Him for help. The Bible tells us that He is close to the brokenhearted (Psalm 34:18).

We may not have the answers we are looking for here in this life, but we can be sure of this: God sees your pain and loves you desperately. Call to Him in times of trouble. If you feel that you're at the end of your rope, look up! His mighty hand is reaching toward you.

Heavenly Father, I feel alone and afraid.
Surround me with Your love and give me peace. Amen.

Help My Unbelief!

"What do you mean, 'If I can'?" Jesus asked. "Anything is possible if a person believes." The father instantly cried out, "I do believe, but help me overcome my unbelief!"

MARK 9:23–24 NLT

- -

This story in the New Testament tells of a man who brought his demon-possessed son to Jesus for healing. First he asked the disciples to drive out the demon, but they could not. Then he said to Jesus, "But if You can do anything, take pity on us and help us."

The man had his focus on his problem instead of on Christ. He was thinking about how long his son had been possessed and the great damage that had been done. He wasn't convinced that Jesus could do anything about it. But Jesus corrected the man and showed him that anything is possible through Christ.

Are you facing hard times right now? Does your faith feel a little weak? When you are tempted to let your problems get the better of you and you feel that your faith isn't strong enough to overcome, pray for God to change your thinking from doubt to firm faith in Christ. And remember, when you are weak, He is strong!

Heavenly Father, my problems seem too big to handle right now. I trust You, and I want to believe that You are bigger than anything I'm facing. Help my unbelief! Amen.

Different Kinds of Love

This is my commandment, That ye love one another, as I have loved you.
JOHN 15:12 KJV

. . . .

Not all love is the same according to the Greek translation of God's Word. For instance, *philia* is defined as a loyalty and friendship for family members or friends. *Eros* is a passionate, sensual desire. *Storge* is a natural affection shown between parent and child.

The one most familiar comes from the word *agape*, meaning not only to have general affection but to hold someone in high regard. The New Testament applies agape love in the relationship between Jesus and His disciples. It is one of self-sacrifice and a giving spirit to all, both friend and foe.

Jesus commands us to love our neighbor as we love ourselves (Matthew 22:39). He doesn't say, "Love your neighbor as long as they keep their dogs from barking or if they maintain their yard and stay on their side of the fence." Rather, He commands us to love as He loves us.

That's God's agape love. It's unconditional and powerful. Agape love builds not destroys; it accepts others' imperfections and is tolerant of people who do things differently than we do.

What's your definition of love? Take some time today and exercise God's love in the same manner He loves you, and see what happens!

Lord, thank You for loving me unconditionally with all of my faults and flaws. Help me to love as I am loved. Amen.

Refreshment in Dry Times

"The grass withers and the flowers fall, but the word of our God endures forever."
ISAIAH 40:8 NIV

. . . .

The grass was lifeless, crunchy, and brown. The trees had already started to lose their leaves, and it was only August. Flowers wilted, and the ground was nothing but dry dirt. The previous winter was unseasonably warm with very little snow. Spring had been practically nonexistent, and summer was day after day of relentless, scorching heat with very little rain. It was a drought with no change in sight.

Sometimes our lives feel just like the grass—dry and listless. Maybe we're in a season where things seem to stand still, and we've tried everything to change our circumstances for the better to no avail. It is during those times that we need to remember the faithfulness of God and the permanence of His Word. His promises to us are many and true! God will never leave us or forsake us; and He will provide for, love, and protect us. And, just like the drought, eventually our personal dry times will give way to a time of growth, refreshment, and beauty.

Dear Lord, help me to remember Your love during
difficult times of dryness. Even though it's sometimes
hard to hear Your voice or be patient during hard times,
please remind me of Your many promises, and remind me
to stand firmly on them. You are everything I need and the
refreshment I seek. Praises to my living water! Amen.

Rejoice!

Rejoice in the Lord always. I will say it again: Rejoice!
PHILIPPIANS 4:4 NIV

• •

Paul wrote Philippians 4:4 from prison. Considering his circumstances, it doesn't seem like he had much reason to rejoice. Yet, he knew what many of us forget: when we have the Lord on our side, we always have reason to rejoice.

He didn't say, "Rejoice in your circumstances." He told us to rejoice in the Lord. When we're feeling depressed, anxious, or lost in despair, we can think of our Lord. We can remind ourselves that we are so very loved. We are special to God. He adores us, and in His heart, each of us is irreplaceable.

Perhaps the reason we lose our joy sometimes is because we've let the wrong things be the source of our joy. If our joy is in our finances, our jobs, or our relationships, what happens when those things fall through? Our joy is lost.

But when God is the source of our joy, we will never lose that joy. Circumstances may frustrate us and break our hearts. But God is able to supply all our needs. He is able to restore broken relationships. He can give us a new job or help us to succeed at our current job. Through it all, despite it all, we can rejoice in knowing that we are God's, and He loves us.

Dear Father, thank You for loving me.
Help me to make You the source of my joy. Amen.

Our prayers
SOFTEN
HARDENED HEARTS
and prepare
THE HEART'S SOIL
TO RECEIVE
God's Word.

Keep Praying

Pray without ceasing.
1 Thessalonians 5:17 KJV

. . . .

E. M. Bounds once said, "Talking to men for God is a great thing, but talking to God for men is greater still." Did you realize that we can passionately witness to someone and never reach that person for Christ until prayer energizes our words?

Perhaps you have a wayward son or daughter, or an unsaved husband. You're heartbroken and have tried to share the message of salvation repeatedly to no avail. You've prayed, but nothing changes. Hoping to open their eyes, you continue to "preach," but soon your preaching becomes nagging and they resist your words all the more. So what should you do? Stop sharing the truth that you know will set them free? Keep silent and hope for the best?

Jesus said, "No one is able to come to Me unless the Father Who sent Me attracts and draws him and gives him the desire to come to Me" (John 6:44 AMPC). Prayer is a prerequisite to salvation. Consistent and passionate prayer for others moves God to draw them through the power of the Holy Spirit. Our prayers soften hardened hearts and prepare the heart's soil to receive God's Word.

It's our job to pray specifically for the needs of a person, and it's God's job to change that person's heart to receive the gospel message.

So don't despair. Just keep praying.

Lord, when I get frustrated and fail to see the results of
my prayers, encourage me to keep praying. Amen.

Mission Impossible

And he said, The things which are impossible with men are possible with God.
LUKE 18:27 KJV

As capable as we may be, some things will always remain impossible for us. No matter how much education we get, how determined we are, or how much money we have, some things are out of our control.

Yet just because something is impossible for us doesn't mean we don't have any hope. Where we can't, God can. The God who created the universe, who set the moon and stars in the sky, who positioned the sun in place, and who brought Lazarus back to life after four days in the grave is a God who knows no limits.

Whatever we face, we can face with confidence. God, who loves us more than anything, will move heaven and earth to fulfill His purpose. And He is a God who likes to show off, who likes to take things to the limit before acting, just so He can get the glory. He is an amazing, all-powerful God, and He cares deeply about each and every one of His children.

It may seem like we are facing the impossible. And left up to us, it may be impossible. But we must never, ever forget. Nothing is impossible with God.

Dear Father, thank You for being a God of miracles.
Help me to trust in Your ability to accomplish Your
purpose, even when it seems impossible to me. Amen.

Hurt Happens–Love Anyway

"I have loved you even as the Father has loved me. Remain in my love."
JOHN 15:9 NLT

· ·

Do you ever feel like Jesus overcame life's challenges more easily than you because He was God? It's important to realize that Jesus lived His life on earth as a man—empowered just as you are today as a believer. He relied on His relationship with God and the Holy Spirit working in Him to do all that He did. He too was human. He suffered pain, hurt, and disappointment just as you do.

Imagine His feelings when brothers, sisters, aunts, uncles, and cousins refused to believe He was the Messiah or discounted His words of truth because He was family. How painful it must have been to have those closest to Him reject Him. Jesus knew that Judas would betray Him and Peter would deny Him. Jesus must have felt that hurt deeply—and yet He loved them anyway. On the cross, He asked God to forgive those who put Him there.

When faced with pain or disappointment, it's easier to become angry, defend yourself, or even sever the relationship. The same Spirit that empowered Jesus to live His faith can empower you. When hurt happens—choose to love anyway!

Lord, You have shown me how to respond in love.
Give me strength by Your Holy Spirit to love others in the
face of pain, disappointment, and hurt. Comfort me and
provide ways for me to show love to others. Amen.

Praying the Mind of Christ

We demolish arguments and every pretension that sets
itself up against the knowledge of God, and we take captive
every thought to make it obedient to Christ.

2 CORINTHIANS 10:5 NIV

As Christ followers, we are learning to become like Him in our thoughts, words, and deeds. Part of becoming Christlike is also in mastering our minds. Sometimes it is hard to pray because other thoughts interfere with our ability to listen closely to what God is saying. This is a favorite trick of Satan's. . . getting us to think about our to-do list instead of what God is trying to tell us.

By reading and praying scripture and using positive statements in our prayers that claim what God has already said He will do for us, the mind of Christ is being activated in us. By taking captive every thought, we learn to know what thought is of God, what belongs to us, and what is of the enemy. Recognize, take captive, and bind the thoughts that are of the enemy, and throw them out! The more we commune with God, fellowship with Him, and learn from Him, the more we cultivate the mind of Christ.

Lord, help me identify the thoughts that are not Your thoughts and purge them. I know that soon Your thoughts will be the ones that I hear, and not the enemy's. In this way, I will hear You more clearly so I may be an obedient disciple. Amen!

Much, Much More

With God's power working in us, God can do much, much more
than anything we can ask or imagine. To him be glory in the church
and in Christ Jesus for all time, forever and ever. Amen.

EPHESIANS 3:20–21 NCV

· ·

Think back to a time when something happened in your life that you never saw coming. Something that happened out of the blue, was not on your radar, and absolutely amazed you. When God's power is at work within you, the possibilities are beyond your imagination.

The New International Version of the Bible says in Ephesians 3:20 that He can do "immeasurably more" than what you could imagine. Whatever problem you are facing right now—big or small—God cares. As you pray about it and seek God's will, don't put Him in a box thinking that there's no way out or that there is only one right answer. His response just might be beyond your understanding and your wildest imagination.

Remember that things aren't always what they seem. When you feel disappointed in God's answers to your prayers, look outside the box. God is always, always working everything out for your good. God sees all. What may feel like the best answer may be totally destructive to you or someone you love. Trust that God can do much more than anything you could ever ask or imagine!

Heavenly Father, help me trust You with my whole heart.
When I'm disappointed, help me to see outside of myself and
what I think are the best answers for my life. Thank You for
working everything out according to Your great plan. Amen.

The Higher Road

"In this world you will have trouble. But take heart! I have overcome the world."
JOHN 16:33 NIV

. . . .

During World War II, the Nazis imprisoned author Dr. Victor Frankl. As the Gestapo stripped him and cut away his wedding band, Frankl thought, *You can take away my wife, my children, and strip me of my clothes and freedom, but there is one thing you cannot take—my freedom to choose how I react to whatever happens to me.*

John 16:33 acknowledges that Jesus overcame the world on our behalf, so we are fully equipped to do the same.

It's difficult to trust God against all odds when problems slash us like a paper shredder. Yet it is during those times that God gives us a clear choice: choose faith or break under the harsh realities of life.

Dr. Frankl had learned somewhere in his life's journey to take the higher road. He knew that faith and how we react to people or problems is a choice, not a feeling. We can respond in the flesh or submit to the Holy Spirit whatever happens to us. Often that means asking for forgiveness though you've done nothing wrong, encouraging someone despite their negative attitude, or extending a hand and risking rejection.

Mature believers know that hardships are a part of life, but Jesus has paved the pathway to overcome. And although taking "the higher road" is less traveled, it's worth the trek.

Lord, whatever I face, may I act, not react,
with Your overcoming power. Amen.

The Love of Strangers

*If anyone has material possessions and sees a brother or
sister in need but has no pity on them, how can the love
of God be in that person? Dear children, let us not love
with words or speech but with actions and in truth.*

1 JOHN 3:17–18 NIV

When we think of hospitality in the modern sense, we often think about
being a good hostess, opening our home to friends and family, perhaps
bringing a housewarming gift to a new neighbor or a covered dish to a family
during an illness. Though all of that is hospitable, the literal meaning of
hospitality in the Greek is "the love of strangers."

As Christ followers, we are called to give generously and sacrificially to
all kinds of people, not just our friends or others that we know. The work
of the Holy Spirit transforms our hearts so that we consider others before
ourselves, sacrificing our time and resources to give others provision and rest.
Exercising true hospitality allows us to use all our gifts for God's kingdom.

Loving Father, thank You for the many gifts You have given me—
time, talent, and financial resources. Show me how You wish me to
use each gift in a generous and hospitable way for Your kingdom.
I pray that You use me to be a rich blessing to others. Amen.

Standing in the Light

*Though I have fallen, I will rise. Though I sit in
darkness, the LORD will be my light.*
MICAH 7:8 NIV

Ever fall so low, you think you'll never get up again? Whether it's a job that's evaporated, a bad medical report, or a failed relationship, life has a way of knocking us down. When that happens, we often feel like we'll never stand again.

But with God, we know the low times aren't the end of our story. We may fall down, but He will lift us up. We may feel surrounded by darkness on every side, but He will be our light, guiding the way, showing us which step to take next. No matter where we are, what we've done, or what we're facing, God is our rescuer, our Savior, and our friend.

Satan wants to convince us that we have no hope, no future. But God's children always have a future and a hope. And someday, when death calls our name, even then we will be victorious. For on that day, we will be ready to experience total love and acceptance. We will know once and for all that we are special, we are cherished, and we belong to Him.

Dear Father, thank You for giving me confidence
in a future filled with good things. When I'm down,
remind me to trust in Your love. Thank You for lifting
me out of darkness to stand in Your light. Amen.

All about Me

*You know me inside and out, you know every bone in my body; you know
exactly how I was made, bit by bit, how I was sculpted from nothing
into something. . . . All the stages of my life were spread out before you,
the days of my life all prepared before I'd even lived one day.*

PSALM 139:15–16 MSG

Have you ever considered how matchless you are in this world? No one is
created in exactly the same way. We each have our own personalities, gifts,
ideas, and dreams. C. S. Lewis wrote, "Why else were individuals created, but
that God, loving all infinitely, should love each differently?"

Accepting our individuality is a lifetime lesson since there will be many
times we will compare ourselves with others. But God has shown His love
through the unique way He creates and guides our lives. We are distinct,
one from another. His presence in our lives keeps us on a path He created
just for us. It's hard to fathom that kind of love.

With that knowledge, we can learn to love ourselves and others with
Christlike love and enrich our relationship with Him. Ever-growing,
ever-learning, we can trust the heavenly Father to mature us into what He
created us to be: "Just ME."

Thank You, Father, for loving me each day.
Keep me on the path You created. Amen.

Recycling

All praise to the God and Father of our Master, Jesus the Messiah. . . .
He comes alongside us when we go through hard times, and before you
know it, he brings us alongside someone else who is going through hard
times so that we can be there for that person just as God was there for us.
2 CORINTHIANS 1:3–4 MSG

Have you ever considered how much use the Lord can make out of the garbage of our lives? As Christians, we can take the good and bad events we've experienced and use them to witness to others of the goodness of God. When we've walked a path and struggled with a problem, and God has seen us through to the other side, we need to reach out to a brother or sister.

Ambassador Clare Boothe Luce once stated, "There are no hopeless situations; there are only people who have grown hopeless about them." That's when we might offer encouragement.

God weaves a life tapestry for each of us; when we focus on the knotted thread, we don't see any beauty. However, a fellow believer can show us his tapestry made from similar knots, and we see the picture. How precious of the Lord to allow us to share with one another. Never underestimate the power of your testimony.

Father, show me this day how You would have me
share what You have done in my life. Amen.

Worry vs. Prayer

Don't worry about anything; instead, pray about everything.
Tell God what you need, and thank him for all he has done.
PHILIPPIANS 4:6 NLT

Do not worry. This is a tall order for women. We are worriers by nature, aren't we? We worry about our children and friends. We worry about what people think of us and what we will do if such-and-such happens. We are the queens of the what-ifs! But the Bible tells us not to worry about *anything*.

In the book of Matthew, we are reminded that if God cares for the birds of the air, providing them with food as they need it, He is certain to take care of His children! But if we give up worrying, what will we do with all the time we spent being anxious? Exchange it for time in prayer. Go before God with your concerns. Cast all your cares on Him, for He promises to care for you. Tell God what you need, and thank Him in advance for what He will do. God will always provide. He will always show up. He does not want you to worry.

Lord, replace my worry time with prayer time. It is in Jesus' name that I come before You now, presenting You with my requests. Thank You for Your provision in my life. Amen.

Thankful, Thankful Heart

I will praise you, LORD, with all my heart.
I will tell all the miracles you have done.
PSALM 9:1 NCV

. . . .

If you live from the perspective that 10 percent of life is what happens to you and 90 percent is how you respond, then every situation has a side—positive or negative. Say you're late to work; every stoplight on your way is a red one; and you feel like you just can't make up the time. Instead of complaining, consider that maybe the delay was one that God appointed to keep you safe.

When you choose to approach life with a positive outlook, you can practice thankfulness in most of life's circumstances. It completely changes your attitude and your countenance. God wants to bless you. When you are tempted to feel sorry for yourself or to blame others or God for difficulties, pause. Take a moment and rewind your life. Look back and count the blessings that God has given you. As you remind yourself of all He has done for you and in you, it will bring change to your attitude and give you hope in the situation you're facing. Count your blessings today.

Lord, I am thankful for my life and all You have done
for me. When life happens, help me to respond to it in a
healthy, positive way. Remind me to look to You and trust
You to carry me through life's challenges. Amen.

WHEN YOU CHOOSE
TO APPROACH LIFE WITH
a positive outlook,
YOU CAN PRACTICE
thankfulness
IN MOST OF LIFE'S
CIRCUMSTANCES.

Blessable

Love the LORD your God and. . .serve him with all your heart and with all your soul—then I will send rain on your land in its season.
DEUTERONOMY 11:13–14 NIV

. . . .

We all want God's blessings. We want it to rain on our crops; we want the sun to shine on our picnics; and we want a gentle breeze to relieve us from summer's scorch. We want job security and bigger paychecks.

Though God allows some blessings to grace every person in the human race, there are some keys to receiving more of God's goodness. If we want God's blessings, we must be blessable.

So how do we become blessable? We must love God. And we must serve Him with all our hearts.

Loving God is the easy part. But the evidence of that love comes through our service to Him, and that's a little harder.

When we love God, we serve Him by loving others. We serve Him by taking the time to mow the widow's lawn or prepare a meal for someone who's ill or provide a coat for someone who's cold. We serve Him by offering a hand of friendship to the friendless or by saying something positive about the victim of gossip.

When we love God and our actions show evidence of that love, we become blessable. That's when God will pour out His goodness on us in ways we could never imagine.

Dear Father, I love You. Show me ways
I can serve You today. Amen.

Thank You, Lord

I will praise the LORD at all times. I will constantly speak his praises.
PSALM 34:1 NLT

. . . .

While imprisoned, the apostle Paul gave thanks to God, even singing His praises, and it resulted in the salvation of the jailers. What a great lesson for every Christian—when you feel least like giving thanks, that's precisely when you should!

What is your response when you find yourself trapped in traffic, late for a meeting, frustrated in your plans, sick in bed, hurting emotionally, overwhelmed with work, lonely, tired, or confused? Our human nature tells us we should gripe and fret. Yet scripture says we should give thanks. Only when we surrender our lives to Him and His control is this possible.

Learn to thank Him. Thank Him for being your help in times of trouble. Thank Him for His great wisdom and power. And thank Him for causing every situation in your life to work together for your good.

Giving thanks may not change your circumstances significantly, but it will change you. You'll feel yourself focusing on God—His goodness, kindness, and grace—rather than your own anger, pride, sickness, or inconvenience. Maybe that's why it's such fertile soil for miracles. The biblical commentator Matthew Henry stated it well: "Thanksgiving is good, but thanks-living is better."

Lord, I choose to give You thanks today for whatever comes my way. I love You, Lord, and I am grateful for Your goodness. Amen.

105

A Friend Who Sticks Closer Than a Brother

When David had finished speaking to Saul, the soul of Jonathan was knit with the soul of David, and Jonathan loved him as his own life.

1 Samuel 18:1 AMPC

. . . .

The relationship between David and Jonathan was like that of brothers. Proverbs 18:24 (NIV) says it this way: "One who has unreliable friends soon comes to ruin, but there is a friend who sticks closer than a brother." Everyone hits a rough patch now and then. This world is not our home. As believers, we are aliens here. One day we will truly be at home in heaven with the Lord. Until then, it is important that we stand strong with one another through the ups and downs of life.

Consider the depth of Jonathan's love for David: Jonathan, the son of King Saul, protected David from death when Saul grew jealous of David. He created a secret way of getting the message to David that he indeed needed to flee the kingdom. The two hated to part, but it was their only option. In the end, the Bible tells us it was David who wept the hardest when he had to leave Jonathan. No doubt, David recognized the value of his true friend who stuck closer than a brother. Do you have a friend in need? Life gets busy. Don't ever be too busy to help your friends, to be there for them as Jonathan was for David.

Father in heaven, may I be a friend who truly
sticks closer than a brother. Amen.

The Gift of Prayer

First of all, then, I admonish and urge that petitions, prayers, intercessions, and thanksgivings be offered on behalf of all men.... For such [praying] is good and right, and [it is] pleasing and acceptable to God our Savior.
1 TIMOTHY 2:1, 3 AMPC

There is such joy in giving gifts. Seeing the delight on someone's face to receive something unexpected is exciting.

Perhaps the absolute greatest gift one person can give to another doesn't come in a box. It can't be wrapped or presented formally, but instead it is the words spoken to God for someone—the gift of prayer.

When we pray for others, we ask God to intervene and to make Himself known to them. We can pray for God's plan and purpose in their lives. We can ask God to bless them or protect them. You can share with them that you are praying for them or do it privately without their knowledge. Who would God have you give the gift of prayer to today?

Lord, thank You for bringing people to my heart and mind
who need prayer. Help me to pray the things that they
need from You in their lives. Show me how to give the gift
of prayer to those You would have me pray for. Amen.

Staying on Track

I have fought a good fight, I have finished my course, I have kept the faith.
2 TIMOTHY 4:7 KJV

· ·

In our hustle-bustle world, it's easy to get so busy we forget our priorities. Hopefully, as believers, we've established our priority list with God at the top. Staying in touch with Him and walking in His will should be our number one goal.

Paul knew this when he exhorted the churches to stick closely to the teachings of Jesus. He knew the fickle heart and how easy it would be for them to stray. In his letters to Timothy, he reminded the young man of the importance of drawing close to God, hearing His heartbeat. Despite the pain and afflictions Paul suffered in his life, he kept his eyes on Jesus, using praise to commune with God.

Likewise, we can keep in constant communion with the Father. We are so blessed to have been given the Holy Spirit within to keep us in tune with His will. Through His guidance, that still, small voice, we can rest assured our priorities will stay focused on Jesus. As the author A. W. Tozer wrote, "Lord, guide me carefully on this uncharted sea as I daily seek You in Your word. Then use me mightily as Your servant this year as I boldly proclaim Your word in leading others."

Lord, no better words have been spoken than
to say I surrender to Your will. Amen.

Perfect Peace

*You will keep in perfect peace all who trust in you, all whose thoughts are fixed
on you! Trust in the LORD always, for the LORD GOD is the eternal Rock.*
ISAIAH 26:3–4 NLT

. . . .

What does perfect peace look like? Is it a life without problems? Is it a smooth
ride into the future without any bumps in the road? Not for the Christian.
We know life on earth won't ever be easy, but God promises to keep us in
perfect peace if our thoughts are fixed on Him.

Perfect peace is only found by having a moment-by-moment relationship with Jesus Christ. It is ongoing faith and trust that God really has it all
figured out. It's believing that each setback, heartbreak, problem, and crisis
will be made right by God.

You can live in peace even during the messy stuff of life. You don't have to
have everything figured out on your own. Doesn't that take some pressure off?

"And the God of all grace, who called you to his eternal glory in Christ,
after you have suffered a little while, will himself restore you and make you
strong, firm and steadfast" (1 Peter 5:10 NIV). That's perfect peace.

Heavenly Father, thank You for offering me peace in the midst of
the stress of this life. Thank You that I'm not in charge and that
You have everything already figured out. I trust You. Amen.

Women of Faith

*I remember your true faith. That faith first lived in your grandmother Lois
and in your mother Eunice, and I know you now have that same faith.*

2 TIMOTHY 1:5 NCV

When the apostle Paul thought of young Timothy, one thing stood out. Timothy had true faith. He had been raised by his mother and grandmother to love and trust the Lord. Perhaps you come from a long line of Christian women, or maybe you are a first-generation Christ follower. Either way, these verses have a message for you. We all influence children. Perhaps you have your own children or nieces and nephews. Maybe you spend time with friends' children. Maybe you're a grandmother. Or you may work with children either in your career or in a church ministry role. Whatever the situation, you have a great impact on children that look up to you.

It is important to note the trait that stood out was not perfection. It was faith. We cannot be perfect examples for our children. But we can teach them about faith! The way you respond to life's trials speaks the loudest. Children learn about faith when they see it lived out before them. Like Eunice and Lois were wonderful examples for Timothy, may you influence the next generation to place their faith in Christ Jesus.

God, help me to be a woman of faith, for I know that little ones
are watching and learning about You through me. Amen.

Casting Cares

Cast all your anxiety on him because he cares for you.
1 PETER 5:7 NIV

. . . .

Do you have tiresome work that beckons, follows, and awaits you? No matter how demanding it is, the way you handle that work can reflect God.

Do you have relationship challenges with a husband, parent, friend, or child? The way you handle those challenges can be a bright spot for everyone involved.

Are you fearful about the future, either for yourself or your children? The way you handle that fear can be a blessing into eternity.

Are there health issues that you or a loved one face? What you do with those can speak to the lives of many.

Do your friends, neighbors, or coworkers have things they are deeply struggling with that they have asked you to pray about or to talk about with them? Listening and praying can make a world of difference for them in so many ways.

Does it seem that there are too many burdens, people, problems, and things to pray for? Give them all to God. He wants to take care of every one.

Lord God, thank You for being the Sovereign Almighty
who can handle all of the cares we have. Amen.

Love and Faithfulness

So the Word became human and made his home among us.
He was full of unfailing love and faithfulness. And we have seen
his glory, the glory of the Father's one and only Son.
JOHN 1:14 NLT

Jesus came in human flesh—fully knowing what would be done to Him—to allow complete access to God. Jesus says that the only way to God is through Him (John 14:6). Before Christ came, one could know about God. Through Jesus, we all can have an intimate relationship with God.

Christ came full of unfailing love and faithfulness. No other relationship can fill you with the love that comes through Jesus. No other relationship can meet all of your needs. No other relationship can be depended on in the way that you can trust God's faithfulness.

Earthly relationships will leave you lacking if you come to count on them for your happiness. People will let you down. It's a guarantee. Even your most trusted loved ones cannot be faithful all the time. But Jesus' love is unfailing. He promises to never leave or forsake you (Hebrews 13:5). Put your faith and trust in the only one who is worthy.

Heavenly Father, I'm eternally grateful that Your love and faithfulness will never leave me. Help me depend fully on Your faithfulness alone, and give me a healthy perspective and balance in my earthly relationships. Amen.

Sending God's Favor

You help us by your prayers. Then many will give thanks on our behalf for the gracious favor granted us in answer to the prayers of many.
2 CORINTHIANS 1:11 NIV

"I'll pray for you." Why is it those words seem weak, almost trite at times? It's what we say when we don't know what to say. When we don't know what to do, but we long to do something.

Yet, those four words are probably the most powerful words we can speak, as long as we follow through. When we pray, we call upon all the power of the King of heaven. When we pray, we see results. When we pray, miracles happen.

When we pray, people are blessed.

Friend, the power of prayer is better in a crisis than a casserole. It's better than being there, holding someone's hand, or doing their laundry. The power of prayer does more for a missionary on the other side of the world than a box of clothes or even a check.

Prayer brings peace. Prayer brings wisdom and clarity. Prayer is powerful.

Next time you offer to pray for someone, you can say it with the confidence that your prayers will be heard. They will be answered. And they will make a beautiful difference in the lives of those for whom you pray.

Dear Father, thank You for hearing my prayers.
Thank You for showing favor to others at my request. Amen.

GOD,

who knows the
thoughts and *intents*
of our hearts,

is well pleased

when we
do what is right,
whether or not
anyone notices.

Please God

For God is pleased when, conscious of his will,
you patiently endure unjust treatment.

1 PETER 2:19 NLT

Few moms hear comments from their children or husband like, "Hey, thanks for washing my basketball uniform," or "I appreciate the way you remind me to do my homework," or "Wow, the toilet bowl is sparkling clean!" Face it. Women just don't receive that kind of encouragement; yet we do those things anyway, with no thought of receiving credit. It's simply what we do for our families.

The same is true as believers. It's always right to do right. Christians serve, give, pray, encourage, and bless others because it is the right thing to do. These actions are as natural to the true believer as escorting a five-year-old across the street is to a mother.

Are you discouraged when no one notices how well you conducted a Bible study or served a church dinner? Does it bother you if your good deeds go unnoticed? Then it's time for a motive check. God, who knows the thoughts and intents of our hearts, is well pleased when we do what is right, whether or not anyone notices.

We serve without applause because we love God, not because we desire to please men. Besides, the only one we should strive to satisfy is our God, who sees what we do in secret and is delighted.

Dear Lord, thank You for the encouragement You give me daily.
Although I don't deserve it, I am deeply grateful for it! Amen.

115

A Forever Love

But I trust in your unfailing love; my heart rejoices in your salvation.
PSALM 13:5 NIV

· ·

The Bible tells us that God's love for us is unfailing. The dictionary defines *unfailing* as "completely dependable, inexhaustible, endless." Our hearts can truly rejoice knowing that we can never exhaust God's love. It won't run out. We can completely depend on God and His love for us at all times and in all situations.

Many people—even Christians—go through life believing that God is just a grumpy old man at the edge of heaven looking down on us with disappointment and disgust. That couldn't be further from the truth! Through Jesus Christ and His power at work within us, God sees us as "*holy* and *dearly loved*" (Colossians 3:12 NIV) children. His love is unfailing, and that can never change! Check out the following verses:

"In your unfailing love you will lead the people you have redeemed. In your strength you will guide them to your holy dwelling" (Exodus 15:13 NIV).

"Many are the woes of the wicked, but the LORD's unfailing love surrounds the one who trusts in him" (Psalm 32:10 NIV).

"How priceless is your unfailing love, O God! People take refuge in the shadow of your wings" (Psalm 36:7 NIV).

The next time you start to think that God is upset with you, remember His unfailing and unchanging love.

Father in heaven, Your unfailing love surrounds me as I trust
in You. Thank You for Your amazing promise! Amen.

At All Times

Pray in the Spirit at all times with all kinds of prayers.
EPHESIANS 6:18 NCV

When giving instructions about important things, it's good to be specific. The more specific the instructions, the more likely the task will be done correctly. That's why when Paul spoke to the Ephesians about praying, he didn't leave any question about when to pray.

Prayer isn't a ritual to practice before bed or first thing in the morning or when the sun is at a certain place in the sky. Though it's great to have specific times of concentrated, focused prayer, our conversations with God shouldn't be limited to a certain time on our clock. God wants us to pray *all the time.*

After all, God wants to be included in our days. He wants to walk and talk with us each moment. Imagine if we traveled through the day with our children or our husband, but we only spoke to them between 6:15 and 6:45 a.m.! Of course we'd never do that to the people we care about. God doesn't want us to do that to Him either.

God wants to travel the journey with us. He's a wonderful companion, offering wisdom and comfort for every aspect of our lives. But He can only do that if we let Him into our schedules, every minute of every day.

Dear Father, thank You for always being there to listen.
Remind me to talk to You about everything, all the time. Amen.

Walk a Mile in the Master's Shoes

For this very reason, make every effort to add to your
faith goodness; and to goodness, knowledge.
2 PETER 1:5 NIV

. . . .

Remember when you bought a new pair of shoes and had to break them in? They tended to pinch the toes a bit. But after a few weeks, they conformed to your foot and became more comfortable. So it is with the Christian life. When we start out on our walk of faith, it's not always a comfortable journey; we try to emulate Christ and His ways, to walk in His shoes, and we need to learn it takes time to get the correct fit.

God, in His infinite grace and mercy, knows we'll stumble. We can place our hope in Him with confidence He'll understand. He's not there with a heavy hand to push us down as we toddle along, new in our spiritual walk. He doesn't look for opportunities to say, "Aha, you messed up!" Quite the contrary: He encourages us with His Word.

For example, we read that the patriarchs in the Bible weren't perfect. Filled with flaws, David was still called a man after God's own heart (1 Samuel 13:14 and Acts 13:22). In the same way, as we grow and learn with the aid of the Spirit, our lives will also reflect more of Him. And as we grow ever more sure-footed, we'll reach our destination—to be like our Father.

Gracious Lord, thank You for Your ever-present guidance. Amen.

Before You Ask

"Seek the Kingdom of God above all else, and live righteously,
and he will give you everything you need."

MATTHEW 6:33 NLT

· ·

"Dear God, please. . ."

Do your prayers begin that way? "Dear God, please help me to be patient with my kids." "Dear God, please heal my friend's illness." "Dear God, please provide enough money to pay this month's bills." God wants believers to ask for whatever they need. But Jesus reminds them that there is a right way to pray, and prayer is more than asking.

In the Lord's Prayer, Jesus teaches His followers how to pray. He begins, "Our Father in heaven, may your name be kept holy. May your Kingdom come soon. May your will be done on earth, as it is in heaven" (Matthew 6:9–10 NLT). First, Jesus honors God's holiness. Next, He shows faith in God's promise of reigning over the earth and redeeming His people. Then He accepts God's perfect will. Praise, faith, and acceptance come before asking. Jesus reminds believers to honor God first, put God's will second, and pray for their own needs third. His prayer begins with God and ends with Him: "For thine is the kingdom, and the power, and the glory, for ever. Amen" (Matthew 6:13 KJV).

Bring your requests to God. Ask specifically and confidently, but remember Jesus' model—put God first in your prayers.

Dear God, I praise You. My faith rests in You,
and I accept whatever Your will is for my life. Amen.

Joyous Light

Whom having not seen, ye love; in whom, though now ye see him not, yet believing, ye rejoice with joy unspeakable and full of glory.
1 PETER 1:8 KJV

Artist Thomas Kinkade was called the "painter of light." His work reflects light shining from the canvas, brightening his pictures. Wouldn't it be wonderful to be known as someone who lightens the places she goes? Most often those who light up a room do so because they contain such a measure of love and joy, often contagious joy. Light-filled people who love the Lord are infectious with a dazzling light illuminating the darkness.

Jesus is the light of the world. When we accept Him, the light is poured into us. The Holy Spirit comes to reside within, bringing His light. A glorious gift graciously given to us. When we realize the importance of the gift and the blessings that result from a life led by the Father, we can't contain our happiness. The joy and hope that fill our hearts well up. Joy uncontained comes when Jesus becomes our Lord. Through Him, through faith, we have hope for the future. What joy! So let it spill forth in love. Be a contagious, light-filled Christian, spreading your hope, joy, and love to a hurting world.

Lord, help me to be a light unto the world,
shining forth Your goodness. Amen.

Encourage Yourself

David encouraged himself in the LORD his God.
1 SAMUEL 30:6 KJV

David and his army went off to fight, leaving their families behind in Ziklag. While they were gone, their enemy the Amalekites raided the city, burned it, and captured the women and children. When the men returned, they found just a smoking pile of rubble. Enraged and weeping uncontrollably, some blamed David and wanted him killed. What did David do when no one was around to encourage him? He encouraged himself in the Lord (1 Samuel 30:1–6).

David had a personal relationship with God. He knew the scriptures, and he relied on God's promises. Instead of giving in to discouragement, he applied those promises to his own situation and found strength. David relied on God to build him up. Many believe that he wrote these words in Psalm 119:15–16: "I will study your commandments and reflect on your ways. I will delight in your decrees and not forget your word" (NLT). *I will delight myself in Your decrees.* In the middle of his grief and loneliness, David delighted himself in the Lord.

Christians never have to face discouragement alone. As they trust God, they can also recall past times when He brought them success. They can communicate with Him through prayer and find support in His Word.

Remember, God is always on your side, always there, and always ready to lift you up.

Dear God, thank You for encouraging me with
Your promises and Your love. Amen.

Honoring Mothers

When Jesus therefore saw his mother, and the disciple standing by, whom he loved, he saith unto his mother, Woman, behold thy son! Then saith he to the disciple, Behold thy mother! And from that hour that disciple took her unto his own home.

JOHN 19:26–27 KJV

Jesus knew the value of a mother. Mary held a special place in His heart. She brought Him into this world. Straight from heaven's glory, He was wrapped in swaddling clothes by Mary's loving hands and laid in a manger bed. Years later, from the cross, in agony, breathing His dying breaths, Jesus made preparations for His mother's care. He told the disciple dearest to His heart, believed to be John, to take Mary as his own mother.

There is a lesson here for all of us. When we are children, our mothers care for us. Inevitably, at some point, the tables turn. Our mothers need our care. Follow the example laid out for you by your Savior. Honor your mother all the days of your life. Honor her by living well, spending time with her, and by meeting any needs she may have. No mother and child relationship is perfect, but God's Word is clear in its command to honor our mothers. Love and serve your mother. . .for this pleases God.

God, help me to honor my mother. May my words and actions bring glory to You as I love my mother well. Amen.

He Carries Us

In his love and mercy he redeemed them. He lifted them
up and carried them through all the years.

Isaiah 63:9 NLT

. . . .

Are you feeling broken today? Depressed? Defeated? Run to Jesus and not away from Him.

When we suffer, He cries. Isaiah 63:9 (NLT) says, "In all their suffering he also suffered, and he personally rescued them. In his love and mercy he redeemed them. He lifted them up and carried them through all the years."

He will carry us—no matter what pain we have to endure. No matter what happens to us. God sent Jesus to be our redeemer. He knew the world would hate, malign, and kill Jesus. Yet He allowed His very flesh to writhe in agony on the cross—so that we could also become His sons and daughters. He loved me, and you, that much.

One day, we will be with Him. "Beloved," He will say, "no more tears. No more pain." He will lift us up and hold us in His mighty arms, and then He will show us His kingdom, and we will, finally, be whole.

Lord Jesus, thank You for coming to us—for not abandoning us when we are broken. Thank You for Your work on the cross, for Your grace, mercy, and love. Help me to seek You even when I can't feel You, to love You even when I don't know all the answers. Amen.

Linking Hearts with God

*"You will receive power when the Holy Spirit comes on you;
and you will be my witnesses. . .to the ends of the earth."*

ACTS 1:8 NIV

God knows our hearts. He knows what we need to make it through a day. So in His kindness, He gave us a gift in the form of the Holy Spirit. As a counselor, a comforter, and a friend, the Holy Spirit acts as our inner compass. He upholds us when times are hard and helps us hear God's directions. When the path of obedience grows dark, the Spirit floods it with light. What revelation! He lives within us. Therefore, our prayers are lifted to the Father, to the very throne of God. Whatever petitions we have, we may rest assured they are heard.

We can rejoice in the fact that God cared enough to bless our lives with the Spirit to direct our paths. God loves the praises of His people, and these praises revive the Spirit within you. If you are weary or burdened, allow the Holy Spirit to minister to you. Seek the Holy Spirit and His wisdom, and ask Him to revive and refresh your inner man. Place your hope in God and trust the Spirit's guidance, and He will never let you down.

Father God, how blessed I am to come into Your presence.
Help me, Father, when I am weak. Guide me this day. Amen.

124

The Power of God's Love

Above all things have intense and unfailing love for one another, for love covers a multitude of sins [forgives and disregards the offenses of others].

1 PETER 4:8 AMPC

Let's face it—we're human. As Christians, we endeavor to follow the teachings of Christ but fall short. Periodically our actions take the course of a runaway train. Maybe a brother tested your patience and your intolerance of his behavior ignited you to lash out in anger. Perhaps a sister in Christ took the credit publicly for some good work you did in private and you seethe. Or maybe someone falsely accused you and you retaliated.

Every believer is flawed, and too often we fail miserably. Peter—endowed with a few flaws of his own—admonished those in the church to love one another intensely. He, above all, had learned the power of repentance and forgiveness, having denied Christ three times after the Roman soldiers apprehended Jesus. Yet Peter was one of the first to see Jesus after His resurrection, and it was Peter who first reached Jesus on the Sea of Galilee. There, the Lord commissioned Peter to feed His sheep. After Jesus' ascension, Peter—the spokesman of the apostles—preached the sermon that resulted in the conversion of about three thousand souls (Acts 2:14–41).

Christ's love forgives and disregards the offenses of others. His love covers a multitude of sins. That's the power of God's love at work. Love resurrects, forgives, restores, and commissions us to reach others for the kingdom.

Jesus, teach me to love rather than to judge. Amen.

125

Love and Mercy

"Therefore, I tell you, her many sins have been forgiven—as her great love has shown. But whoever has been forgiven little loves little."
LUKE 7:47 NIV

The woman in Luke 7 recognized who Jesus was and washed His feet with her perfume. The Bible says that she lived a sinful life but that her faith in Christ saved her. She, who was guilty of much, was forgiven much. She experienced amazing grace and undeserved mercy. She loved Jesus and did what she could to worship Him.

Have you ever received a speeding ticket? Then you most likely deserved it. But have you ever deserved a speeding ticket and the officer let you off the hook? What a huge relief! That's mercy. The Bible tells us that the punishment for sin is death, but the gift of God is eternal life (Romans 6:23). The sinful woman didn't deserve mercy, and neither do we. But through Christ, we have been forgiven much.

God's Word says that if you've been given much, much is expected (Luke 12:48). This applies to many situations. Have you been given love and mercy? Yes, indeed! Then you're expected to show love and mercy in return.

Dear Jesus, I don't deserve what You have done for me.
Help me to remember how much I've been forgiven so that
I can extend that love and mercy to others. Amen.

Ask in Faith

But when you ask God, you must believe and not doubt. Anyone who doubts is like a wave in the sea, blown up and down by the wind.

JAMES 1:6 NCV

. . . .

What does it mean to ask God for something *in faith?* Does it mean we believe that He *can* grant our requests? That He *will* grant our requests? Exactly what is required to prove our faith?

These are difficult questions. Many who have prayed for healed bodies and healed relationships have received exactly that, this side of heaven. Others who have prayed for the same things, believing only God could bring healing, haven't received the answers they wanted.

There is no secret ingredient that makes all our longings come to fruition. The secret ingredient, if there is one, is faith that God is who He says He is. It's faith that God is good and will use our circumstances to bring about His purpose and high calling in our lives and in the world.

When we don't get the answers we want from God, it's okay to feel disappointed. He understands. But we must never doubt His goodness or His motives. We must stand firm in our belief that God's love for us will never change.

Dear Father, I know that You are good and that You love me. I know Your love for me will never change, even when my circumstances are hard. Help me cling to Your love, even when You don't give the answers I want. Amen.

When You Give Your Life Away

Which of you, intending to build a tower, sitteth not down first,
and counteth the cost, whether he have sufficient to finish it?
LUKE 14:28 KJV

Henry David Thoreau once said, "The price of anything is the amount of life you exchange for it." Busy lives often dictate that there is no time for the important things. People say, "Oh, I don't have time for this or that," or "I wish I had the time. . ." The truth is you make the time for what you value most.

Every person has the same amount of time each day. What matters is how you spend it. It's easy to waste your life doing insignificant things—what many call time wasters—leaving little time for God. The most important things in life are eternal endeavors. Spending time in prayer to God for others. Giving your life to building a relationship with God by reading His Word and growing in faith. Sharing Christ with others and giving them the opportunity to know Him. These are the things that will last.

What are you spending your life on? What are you getting out of what you give yourself to each day?

Heavenly Father, my life is full. I ask that You give me wisdom and instruction to give my life to the things that matter most. The time I have is precious and valuable. Help me to invest it wisely in eternal things. Amen.

THE TIME I HAVE IS
precious
AND
valuable.
HELP ME TO INVEST
IT WISELY IN
ETERNAL THINGS.
Amen.

The Hand of God

*"For I am the LORD your God who takes hold of your right
hand and says to you, Do not fear; I will help you."*
ISAIAH 41:13 NIV

. . . .

If there is a scripture you need to have close in times of trouble, this is it!
Post it on your fridge; write it on a sticky note to tack up in your car; commit
it to memory so that the Spirit of God can bring it to mind when you need
to hear it most.

Psalm 139 tells us that God created us and knows everything about us.
He knows when we sit and when we get up, and He knows every word that's
on our tongue before we speak it. Psalm 139:7–10 tells us that no matter
where we go, His hand will guide us and hold us.

Heading to the emergency room? Repeat Isaiah 41:13 and remember that
God is holding your hand. Afraid of the future? Stop worrying and trust the
God who loves you and has great plans for you. Facing a problem that you
cannot possibly bear? Take hold of God's mighty hand and believe that He
will help you.

Father God, help me not to fear. Take hold of my hand and
guide me. I put my faith and trust in You alone. Amen.

Grace Accepted

*Because of his great love for us, God, who is rich in mercy,
made us alive with Christ even when we were dead in
transgressions—it is by grace you have been saved.*

EPHESIANS 2:4–5 NIV

Have you ever been wrongly accused of something or completely misunderstood? Have the words of your accusers struck your heart, making you feel like you have to make it right somehow, but no amount of reasoning with them seems to help?

If anyone understands this situation it's Christ Himself. Wrongly accused. Misunderstood. Yet He offered unfathomable grace at all times and still offers it today.

This reminds us that we are to aim to offer this same grace to our accusers and those who misunderstand us. We will be misunderstood when we try to obey and follow God in a culture that runs quite contrary in many ways. Our job is to first accept God's grace and then offer it up to others as lovingly as we can. Like Christ.

God, help us to continually accept Your grace through Christ and reflect You by offering that same grace to others. Amen.

Like Little Children

Some people brought their little children to Jesus so he could touch them, but his followers told them to stop. When Jesus saw this, he was upset and said to them, "Let the little children come to me. Don't stop them, because the kingdom of God belongs to people who are like these children. I tell you the truth, you must accept the kingdom of God as if you were a little child, or you will never enter it."
MARK 10:13–15 NCV

Have you ever heard a child pray from his heart? Not just a memorized prayer that he repeats before lunch but a real, honest prayer? A four-year-old boy prayed this: "Dear God, I really don't like all the bad dreams I've been having. Will You please make them stop?"

His prayer was so pure and honest. He prayed, believing that God would listen to his prayer and do something about it. He wasn't afraid to say how he really felt.

This passage in Mark tells us that no matter how old we are, God wants us to come to Him with the faith of a child. He wants us to be open and honest about our feelings. He wants us to trust Him wholeheartedly, just like little kids do.

As adults we sometimes play games with God. We tell God what we think He wants to hear, forgetting that He already knows our hearts! God is big enough to handle your honesty. Tell Him how you really feel.

Father, help me come to You as a little child and be more open and honest with You in prayer. Amen.

God's Promises

"God is not human, that he should lie, not a human being, that he should change his mind. Does he speak and then not act? Does he promise and not fulfill?"
NUMBERS 23:19 NIV

Our opinions of God are often shaped by our experiences with people. When we've been hurt, we see God as hurtful. When people lie to us, we subconsciously think of God as a liar. After all, if humans are created in His image, it only stands to reason that God would be like the people in our lives. Right?

Well, no. Yes, we were created in God's image. But we humans are a fallen, broken race. We're sinful. God is without sin.

Humans lie. God doesn't.

Humans go back on their word. God doesn't.

Humans can be mean and hurtful. God is love, and He only acts in love.

God promised good things to those who love Him, those who live and act according to His will. That doesn't mean others won't hurt us or that we won't experience the effects of living in a sin-infested world. But where there's pain, we have a healer. Where there's brokenness, we have a comforter. And where we feel alone, we know we have a friend.

And one day we'll experience the perfect fulfillment of all His promises without the burdens of this world to weigh us down.

Now that's something to look forward to.

Dear Father, thank You for Your promises. When I feel
discouraged, help me to remember those promises. Amen.

Without Love

If I speak in the tongues of men or of angels, but do not have love, I am only a resounding gong or a clanging cymbal.

1 CORINTHIANS 13:1 NIV

Without love, all the good deeds in the world are just a bunch of noise! Like resounding gongs or clanging cymbals, the Pharisees of Jesus' day went about their good works. Over and over, they repeated them. They were duties, not desires of the heart. They based everything on ritual rather than relationship. Are there Pharisees among us today? Certainly! Our job as Christ followers is to show the world the love of God. We do this with open hearts and open arms. We do it in the workplace, in the marketplace, and in our homes. We do it as we come and go; with our children and with other people's children; with our husbands, neighbors, and coworkers. The world desperately needs to see extravagant love in us, love that cannot be explained by any means other than that we walk with the author and creator of love. Don't go about your good deeds out of guilt or so that someone will notice how nice you are. Do good deeds so that others will notice Jesus in you and glorify your Father who is in heaven. Do good deeds out of love. It will always come back to you tenfold.

Lord Jesus, give me opportunities to love this world
so that others might see You in me. Amen.

Loving Sisters

*But Ruth replied, "Don't urge me to leave you or to turn back
from you. Where you go I will go, and where you stay I will stay.
Your people will be my people and your God my God."*

RUTH 1:16 NIV

The story of Ruth and Naomi is inspiring on many levels. It tells of two women from different backgrounds, generations, ethnicity, and even religion. But rather than being obstacles to loving friendship, these differences became invisible. Both women realized that their commitment, friendship, and love for each other surpassed any of their differences. They were a blessing to each other.

Do you have girlfriends who would do almost anything for you? A true friendship is a gift from God. Those relationships provide us with love, companionship, encouragement, loyalty, honesty, understanding, and more! Lasting friendships are essential to living a balanced life.

Father God, thank You for giving us the gift of friendship.
May I be the blessing to my girlfriends that they are to me.
Please help me to always encourage and love them and to
be a loving support for them in both their trials and their
happiness. I praise You for my loving sisters! Amen.

Love Your Neighbor as Yourself

*"'You must love the LORD your God with all your heart,
all your soul, all your mind, and all your strength.'
The second is equally important: 'Love your neighbor as
yourself.' No other commandment is greater than these."*
MARK 12:30–31 NLT

Look out for number one. It is the message this world sends every day in a million ways. We are bombarded with it. If it feels good, do it. Do what is right for you. But is this the message of God's Word? Nothing could be further from the truth!

We are told to love our neighbors as ourselves. As you would treat your own body, your own heart, treat your neighbor the same. But who is your neighbor? Your neighbor is anyone within your sphere of influence. Those who live near you, certainly. But your neighbors also include your coworkers, friends, relatives, and even strangers on the street. When you make a purchase at a convenience store, treat the clerk as you would like to be treated. When you order dinner at a restaurant, imagine how hard the waitress is working. Treat her with kindness.

Consider others even as Christ considered you on the cross. The greatest commandment of all is to love God, and this goes hand in hand with the second commandment. Love one another. Love your neighbor as yourself.

Lord, remind me that my neighbors are all around me.
Teach me to love others as I love myself. Amen.

Side by Side

*Have no fear of sudden disaster or of the ruin that
overtakes the wicked, for the LORD will be at your side
and will keep your foot from being snared.*
PROVERBS 3:25–26 NIV

Our world today is crammed with grim news. Television and Internet reports blast us with every detail of a disaster, often filling our hearts with dread. From the pulpit we hear "perfect love casts out fear." However, we frequently remain apprehensive. There are things of which we must be aware, but we do not need to become overtaken with fear and worry. For the Lord our God has given us a promise in His Word. He is at our side.

The Lord sees the concerns and dreads of His children and has surrounded us with His love. When we gaze into His face and seek His presence, the light of His love will flood any dark corners, dispelling the anxious thoughts and scary shadows. His hand is there to hold us close, allowing us to feel His heartbeat.

As a boat casts off its tether from the dock, we need to cast off the ties to fear and worry and drift upon the sea of peace offered by our heavenly Father. He is at our side and will keep us safe, for He is true love.

Father, this day I surrender my cares to You,
for I know You love me. Amen.

God Has Not Forgotten

Then said he unto me, Fear not, Daniel: for from the first day that thou didst set thine heart to understand, and to chasten thyself before thy God, thy words were heard, and I am come for thy words.

DANIEL 10:12 KJV

Sometimes it seems God is silent. When you pray and ask God to intervene in a situation or help you with a difficulty and you don't hear back right away, there is a temptation to interpret that as God is inactive. The truth is He is never too busy to hear you.

Daniel had great concern for his people. He spent weeks fasting and praying, and he desperately wanted direction—an answer for his people. Imagine being fervently on your knees for three weeks, fasting and praying and *nothing*! Some would have given up and maybe even assumed that God had forgotten. Three weeks pass and an angel comes to let Daniel know that God heard his prayer and went to work the very hour he spoke it.

What are you on your knees before God about? What have you asked Him to do on your behalf? Know that God has not forgotten you. He is working behind the scenes to bring about good in your life. He has the answer you need. Hold on to Him, and believe He will come through for you.

Lord, help me hold on to You, believing that
my answer is on the way. Amen.

Three Strings

Two people are better than one, because they get more done by working together. If one falls down, the other can help him up. But it is bad for the person who is alone and falls, because no one is there to help. . . . A rope that is woven of three strings is hard to break.

ECCLESIASTES 4:9–10, 12 NCV

God uses His people to encourage and strengthen one another. As iron sharpens iron, so a friend sharpens a friend (Proverbs 27:17). We get more accomplished in our own lives—and in the grand scheme of things—when we are open to the help and encouragement of others.

If you see a friend in need of physical, emotional, or spiritual help—ask the Lord to give you the wisdom and understanding to be used in helpful ways. And when a friend offers similar help to you, don't be too proud to accept it.

Ask the Lord to guide you in finding a "three-string" accountability partner. Look for a Christian woman with a strong faith in the Lord who is willing to pray with you, encourage you in your faith, and be honest about your strengths and weaknesses. Meet together regularly and ask each other the hard questions: Were you faithful to the Lord this week? Did you gossip? Is there anything you're struggling with right now? How can I pray for you?

With God, you, and a trusted Christian friend working together, you become a rope of three strings that is hard to break!

Father, thank You for using Your people to encourage and sharpen me. Guide me as I seek an accountability partner who will help me grow in my relationship with You. Amen.

WHEN YOU
FIND YOURSELF
UP AGAINST
A TRIBULATION
THAT SEEMS
INSURMOUNTABLE,

look up.

CHRIST IS THERE.

Strength in the Lord

The LORD is my light and my salvation—whom shall I fear?
The LORD is the stronghold of my life—of whom shall I be afraid?
PSALM 27:1 NIV

Even when it seems that everything is piling up around you, Christ is there for you. Take heart! He is your stronghold, a very present help right in the midst of your trial. Regardless of what comes against you in this life, you have the Lord on your side. He is your light in the darkness and your salvation from eternal separation from God. You have nothing to fear.

At times, this world can be a tough, unfair, lonely place. Since the fall of man in the garden, things have not been as God originally intended. The Bible assures us that we will face trials in this life, but it also exclaims that we are more than conquerors through Christ who is in us! When you find yourself up against a tribulation that seems insurmountable, *look up.* Christ is there. He goes before you, stands with you, and is backing you up in your time of need. You may lose everyone and everything else in this life, but nothing has the power to separate you from the love of Christ. Nothing.

Jesus, I cling to the hope I have in You. You are
my rock, my stronghold, my defense. I will not
fear, for You are with me always. Amen.

Continue in His Love

I have loved you, [just] as the Father has loved Me;
abide in My love [continue in His love with Me].
JOHN 15:9 AMPC

. . . .

What does it mean to "continue" or "remain" in Christ's love? Since His love is perfect, and was shown in the flesh, remaining in His love means staying connected to the person of Jesus Christ through the priceless gift of His Spirit.

Throughout your day, ask God to give you creative ways to stay connected to Jesus. Here are a few examples:

When you get up and walk to the coffee maker, pray that God will pour His love into you so that you can pour it into others.

During your shower, ask God to cleanse you of your sins.

As you put on your makeup or style your hair, meditate on His beauty and goodness. Ask Him to make you aware of the beauty He gives through creation and other people throughout the day.

As you eat meals, praise God for the food He gives us in His Word. Take time to meditate on scripture, even if it's just for a few moments, as you eat. If you eat with others, pray for opportunities to talk about Him.

Jehovah God, I praise You for being my creator, redeemer,
and friend. Thank You for giving me the love of Jesus,
and help me to remain in that love every day. Amen.

Making Allowances

Always be humble and gentle. Be patient with each other,
making allowance for each other's faults because of your love.
EPHESIANS 4:2 NLT

This verse contains such a simple, forgotten truth, doesn't it? God wants us to be holy. He wants us to be righteous and good and godly. But He knows we'll never get it exactly right until we're made perfect in His presence.

Until then, we all have our faults. Numerous faults, if we're honest with ourselves. And God doesn't want us standing around, whispering and pointing self-righteous fingers of condemnation. God is the only one who is allowed to wear the judge's robe. The only one.

And He doesn't condemn us. Instead, He pours His love and acceptance into our lives, with a gentle admonition to "go and sin no more" (John 8:11 NLT). In other words, "It's okay. You messed up, but it's been taken care of. The price has been paid. I still love you. Just try not to do it again."

Why do we find it so hard to extend grace to others, when so much grace has been shown to us? As we go through each day, let's make it a point to live out this verse. Let's be humble, gentle, and patient, making allowances for the faults of others because of God's love.

Dear Father, help me to be gentle and loving with others.
Remind me of the grace You've shown me, and help me
show the same love to those around me. Amen.

Deep Roots

"They will be like a tree planted by the water that sends out its roots by the stream. It does not fear when heat comes; its leaves are always green. It has no worries in a year of drought and never fails to bear fruit."
JEREMIAH 17:8 NIV

Watering your garden doesn't seem difficult, but did you know you can train a plant to grow incorrectly, just in the way you water it? By pouring water from the hose for only a few moments at each plant, the root systems become very shallow. They start to seek water from the top of the soil, and the roots can easily be burned in the summer sun. By using a soaker hose, the water slowly percolates into the ground, and the plants learn to push their roots deeper into the soil to get water.

Jeremiah talked about a larger plant, a tree. A tree needs deep roots to keep it anchored in the ground, providing stability. The roots synthesize water and minerals for nourishment and then help to store those elements for a later time. Our deep spiritual roots come from reading God's Word, which provides stability, nourishment, and refreshment.

Father, I do not want to wither in the sun. Help me to immerse myself in Your Word. When I do, I strike my spiritual roots deeper into life-giving soil and drink from living water. Help me to be the fruitful follower of You that I am meant to be. Amen.

The Simple Things

In him our hearts rejoice, for we trust in his holy name.
PSALM 33:21 NIV

. . . .

Think about the simple pleasures in everyday life—that first sip of coffee in the morning, waking up to realize you still have a few more minutes to sleep, or putting on fresh, warm clothes right out of the dryer on a cold winter morning. Perhaps it's a walk along the beach or a hike up the mountains into the blue skies that gives you a simple peace.

God knows all the simple pleasures you enjoy—and He created them for your delight. When the simple things that can come only by His hand fill you with contentment, He is pleased. He takes pleasure in you. You are His delight. Giving you peace, comfort, and a sense of knowing that you belong to Him is a simple thing for Him.

Take a moment today and step away from the busyness of life. Take notice and fully experience some of those things you enjoy most. Then share that special joy with Him.

Lord, thank You for the simple things that bring pleasure
to my day. I enjoy each gift You've given me. I invite You
to share those moments with me today. Amen.

Encourage Others

Worry weighs a person down; an encouraging word cheers a person up.
PROVERBS 12:25 NLT

When was the last time you offered an encouraging word to someone? This can be done in many ways. It can take the form of a card or an email. It can be spoken privately or publicly. Get creative in how you encourage those around you! Write a note of encouragement and put it in your child's lunch box. Stick a note on your husband's steering wheel or briefcase. Place a piece of gum or a miniature chocolate bar on a coworker's desk along with a note of specific encouragement. It only takes a moment, but as Proverbs says, it cheers up the recipient's heart. There is so much sorrow in this world. At any given time, there are many people within your sphere of influence who are hurting. Worry weighs them down as they face disappointment, loss, and other trials. Think about how much it means to you when someone takes the time to encourage you. Do the same for others. Be the voice of encouragement. There is blessing to be found in lifting up those around you.

Father, as I go through this week, make me an encourager.
Provide opportunities for me to encourage those around me. I truly
desire to cheer up the hearts of those who are worried. Amen.

Whispers in the Wind

Then Jesus told him, "Because you have seen me, you have believed;
blessed are those who have not seen and yet have believed."

JOHN 20:29 NIV

. . . .

The wind blew hard, as a good, old-fashioned midwestern rainstorm descended on the town. Trees bent over, their limbs thrashing about. Leaves scattered across yards, and the wind chime clanged a raucous song instead of the gentle, soothing one normally heard.

The wind is invisible. We can feel it as it crosses our skin. We can sometimes smell it as it transports a scent. We can't see *it*, but we can see the effect it has with the blowing leaves. It is powerful. The wind is very much like our faith in God.

We can't see Him. We can't take Him by the hand or even converse with Him face-to-face like we do a friend. But we still know He is present in our lives because we can experience the effects.

God moves among His people, and we can see it. God speaks to His people, and we can hear the still, small voice. And, just like we can feel the wind across our cheeks, we can feel God's presence. We don't need to physically see God to know that He exists and that He's working.

You are like the wind, Lord. Powerful and fast moving,
soft and gentle. We may not see You, but we can sense
You. Help us to believe, even when we can't see. Amen.

The Gift of Encouragement

We have different gifts.... If it is to encourage, then give encouragement.
ROMANS 12:6, 8 NIV

As a Christian, what is the inward desire of your heart? To witness? To serve? To teach? In the book of Romans, Paul lists the different gifts God gives His children according to His grace. These gifts of grace are inward desires and abilities used to further the kingdom of God. Encouragement is one of those gifts.

Have you ever met someone who seems to have the right thing to say at just the right time? Intuitively, she notices when someone is troubled and proceeds to listen and speak words to uplift and encourage.

Paul spoke of encouraging as a God-given desire to proclaim God's Word in such a way that it touches hearts to move them to receive the gospel. Encouragement is a vital part to witnessing because encouragement is doused with God's love. For the believer, it stimulates our faith to produce a deeper commitment to Christ. It brings hope to the disheartened or defeated soul. It restores hope.

Perhaps you are wondering what "gift" you possess. The Bible promises us that every true believer is endowed with at least one or more spiritual gifts (1 Corinthians 12). How will you know your gift? Ask God, and then follow the desires He places on your heart.

Father, help me tune in to the needs of those around
me so that I might encourage them for the gospel's
sake for Your glory and their good. Amen.

The Difference
Barnabas Made

Barnabas accepted Saul and took him to the apostles. . . . Then he told them how boldly Saul had preached in the name of Jesus in Damascus. And so Saul stayed with the followers, going everywhere in Jerusalem, preaching boldly in the name of the Lord.
ACTS 9:27–28 NCV

Did you know that the man we know as Barnabas was not given that name at birth? His name was Joseph. The apostles later gave him the name Barnabas, which means "one who encourages." Isn't it apparent why he was given this name? Barnabas was an encourager.

When Saul literally "saw the light" on the road to Damascus and instantaneously was converted, there were many who did not believe it. Saul had been a Jew among Jews, a Pharisee, a murderer of Christ followers. The apostles did not want to accept him. They were skeptical. But Barnabas stood up for Saul. He testified to the change of heart he had witnessed in the man. Barnabas not only encouraged Saul, but he encouraged the apostles to accept him as a brother in the Lord. Did this encouragement make a difference? Indeed it did. It caused the apostles to accept Saul into the fold. He went throughout Jerusalem with them, preaching Christ as Savior. You never know when a bold word of encouragement may make all the difference in the world.

God, use me as an encourager in this world.
Allow my bold words of encouragement to make
a difference in the lives of others. Amen.

Wait Expectantly

Listen to my voice in the morning, LORD. Each morning
I bring my requests to you and wait expectantly.
PSALM 5:3 NLT

· ·

Why would the psalmist say he waits *expectantly* when praying to the Lord each morning? Perhaps it is because he had seen God answer prayers time and time again! When we develop a habit of prayer, of seeking God and presenting Him with our deepest needs, we also learn to expect Him to answer. When we pray, God listens. He shows up. He never fails to hear His children.

Think about a baby who cries out in the night. The baby learns to expect a parent to come and lift him out of the crib to provide comfort, food, or a dry diaper. Babies in orphanages often stop crying. No one comes when they cry. There is no use. The expectation for rescue and provision wanes. Your heavenly Father is eager and ready to meet with you when you come before Him in prayer. The Bible tells us that His eyes are always roaming across the earth, searching for those who are after His own heart. When you lift your requests to the Sovereign God, rest assured that He is ready to answer. Wait expectantly!

Lord, thank You that You are a God who hears
my prayers and answers. Thank You in advance
for all that You are doing in my life. Amen.

Sincere Love

Love must be sincere. Hate what is evil; cling to what is good.
ROMANS 12:9 NIV

The words *I love you* come easily for some people; for others, those words are withheld and only shared sparingly. As important as those three little words are, they're not nearly as important as the actions behind the words.

Sincere love clings to what is good. Sincere love always protects. It is always patient and kind. It always seeks to bring honor to others. Sincere love always builds up and never tears down.

Some families tell each other they love each other frequently. Yet they gossip and slander and backbite. They seek to dishonor one another at every opportunity. They harm each other's spirits and break each other's hearts. Their words of love aren't sincere.

Others speak the words less frequently, but their actions show kindness and love. The words they do speak bring honor; they build one another up and find ways of showing their love through action.

The words *I love you* are important; we need to hear them. But they ring shallow when they're not backed up with sincere, loving motives and actions. Let's work to show sincere love—backed by actions—to the people God has placed in our lives.

Dear Father, help me to love sincerely. Help me to recognize evil, hurtful motives in my heart. I want to cling to what is good and love others with my words and my actions. Amen.

Loving the Unlovable

"You have heard the law that says, 'Love your neighbor' and hate your enemy. But I say, love your enemies! Pray for those who persecute you! In that way, you will be acting as true children of your Father in heaven."
MATTHEW 5:43–45 NLT

Most of us have family members or people in our lives who are difficult to love. Those people that we would rather not run into in the store so we dart down another aisle hoping they'll check out before we do. You may have one person in your life like that, or many. Difficult people may surround us at every turn. But it's important not to go out of your way to avoid those people. Sometimes running into a difficult person can actually be a "divine appointment"! Maybe you're the only person they'll see all week who wears a smile on her face.

When you happen upon a difficult person whom you'd rather not talk to, take the time to pray for your attitude and then pray for that person. Greet her with a smile and look her in the eye. There is no reason to fear difficult people if you trust in God. He will show you what to do and say as you listen to His promptings (Luke 12:12).

Heavenly Father, I pray that You would help me not to shy away from the people You have allowed to cross my path. Help me speak Your truth and share Your love boldly. Amen.

Two Small Coins

"I tell you the truth," Jesus said, "this poor widow has given more than all the rest of them. For they have given a tiny part of their surplus, but she, poor as she is, has given everything she has."

LUKE 21:3–4 NLT

Financial giving seems like a pretty simple transaction. Some person or organization has a need and others give to fill the need. It's opening up a wallet and removing bills, it's swiping a card or tapping an app, or in a rare occasion it's trying to remember the proper way to write a check. Not much different from any other time currency changes hands, right?

But Jesus doesn't just want our cold, hard cash. He wants our hearts to be involved. A generous spirit that honors God, Jesus says, gives sacrificially. It's stretching ourselves to give out of gratefulness for what God has provided, whether we have much or little.

When it comes down to it, God owns it all anyway, and we are merely the caretakers of His resources. So the next time an opportunity to give arises, ask the supplier what He wants you to give. He can use and will use you in a mighty way!

Generous supplier of my needs, forgive me when I act
like my money is solely mine to hoard and squander.
I want the resources You've blessed me with to be used to
further Your kingdom. Show me how and where. Amen.

Hope in Hopeless Times

Let us hold unswervingly to the hope we profess,
for he who promised is faithful.
HEBREWS 10:23 NIV

Every day the news is filled with reports of the world gone awry and good news is seldom found. Far too many friends are dying, diagnosed to die, or divorcing. Kids in the neighborhood are left alone to care for themselves and resort, all too often, to illegal activities.

In a world deeply steeped with sin, we can look at it two ways: We can feel hopeless and unable to make a difference and do nothing, feeling all is futile. Or we can see that there is endless opportunity to impact the hurting world around us with the love of Christ and the hope He offers.

One church in Ohio sends a group of people to downtown Toledo to sit and talk with people in need on the streets. Tutoring volunteers in a nearby city encourage children in multiple ways with schoolwork and life. A college ministry in another local city makes pancakes in a yard near downtown bars to care for people and invite them to church. One woman takes cookies to her neighbors just for a chance to know them better.

What might you do to make a difference in your neighborhood and town?

God, help us to not lose hope; rather, enable us to love
people and seek to make a difference for You. Amen.

154

There is endless
opportunity
to impact the
hurting world
around us with
the love of Christ
and the hope
He offers.

Breath of Life

He heals the brokenhearted and binds up their wounds
[curing their pains and their sorrows].
PSALM 147:3 AMPC

As a result of sin, every person on the earth is born into a fallen world. The sinful condition brings hurt and heartache to all men—those who serve the Lord and those who don't. The good news is, as a child of God, you have a hope and eternal future in Christ. Jesus said, "I have told you all this so that you may have peace in me. Here on earth you will have many trials and sorrows. But take heart, because I have overcome the world" (John 16:33 NLT).

When your life brings disappointment, hurt, and pain that are almost unbearable, remember that you serve the one who heals hearts. He knows you best and loves you most. When the wind is knocked out of you and you feel like there is no oxygen left in the room, let God provide you with the air you need to breathe. Breathe out a prayer to Him and breathe in His peace and comfort today.

Lord, be my breath of life, today and always. Amen.

Staying Close

"Be strong and courageous. Do not be afraid; do not be discouraged,
for the LORD your God will be with you wherever you go."
JOSHUA 1:9 NIV

. . . .

It's easy to tell others not to worry. It's easy to remind our friends that God is with them and He's got everything under control. And it's easy to remind ourselves of that, when everything's going smoothly.

But when life sails us into rough waters, our natural instinct is to be afraid. We worry and fret. We cry out, not knowing how we will pay the bills or how we will face the cancer or how we will deal with whatever stormy waves crash around us. When life is scary, we get scared.

And believe it or not, that's a good thing. Because when we are afraid, when we are overwhelmed, when we realize that our circumstances are bigger than we are, that's when we're in the perfect place for God to pour out His comfort and assurance on us.

He never leaves us, but sometimes when life is good, we get distracted by other things and don't enjoy His presence as we should. When we feel afraid, we are drawn back to our heavenly Father's arms. And right in His arms is exactly where He wants us to be.

Dear Father, thank You for staying with me and giving me courage.
Help me to stay close to You, in good times and bad. Amen.

High Expectations

"They found grace out in the desert. . .Israel, out looking for a place to rest, met God out looking for them!" God told them, "I've never quit loving you and never will. Expect love, love, and more love!"
JEREMIAH 31:2–3 MSG

Grace out in the desert. What a refreshing thought. Have you been in a desert place, lost, lonely, disappointed, feeling the pain of rejection? Often our immediate response is to berate ourselves, look within to see how we have been the one lacking, plummeting our self-esteem. Dejected, we crawl to that desert place to lick our wounds.

Behold! God is in our desert place. He longs to fill our dry hearts with His healing love and mercy. Yet it's so hard for us—with our finite minds—to grasp that the Creator of the universe cares for us and loves us with an everlasting love, no matter what.

Despite their transgressions, God told the Israelites He never quit loving them. That is true for you today. Look beyond any circumstances and you will discover God looking at you, His eyes filled with love. Scripture promises an overwhelming, unexpected river of love that will pour out when we trust the Lord our God. Rest today in His Word. Expect God's love, love, and more love to fill that empty place in your life.

Father, we read these words and choose this day
to believe in Your unfailing love. Amen.

Pray Expectantly

But when you ask, you must believe and not doubt, because the one who doubts is like a wave of the sea, blown and tossed by the wind.
JAMES 1:6 NIV

. . . .

Do you pray expecting God to answer? George Müller did. Müller was a nineteenth-century evangelist known for his faith in prayer. He studied the Bible and trusted in God's promises. Müller documented fifty thousand answers to prayer, giving credit to his meditation on the scriptures and unbending faith in God. The answers to some of his prayers came in less than twenty-four hours, and others took much persistence and waiting. By faith, Müller trusted God to provide an answer without him asking for anyone's help. He wanted to prove that God is faithful and that He hears when people pray.

George Müller's prayers were rooted in faith. His example suggests that the one who prays must be willing for God to answer in His own time, in His own way, and by His own power. The latter was at the center of Müller's prayers. Instead of trying to find the answer himself, Müller relied on God alone. He opened his heart to God's answer, whatever it was, and he trusted God to answer according to His plan.

Prayer takes faith, persistence, and a willingness to let God have His own way. Try praying daily with that in mind, and expect God to answer.

Father, I trust that You will answer my prayers in a way
that is best for me and most useful to You. Amen.

159

A Good Morsel

Taste and see that the Lord is good; blessed is the one who takes refuge in him.
PSALM 34:8 NIV

Parents sometimes have to encourage children to eat foods they may not even want to try. This may be because of the way it looks, smells, or because they've gotten the notion it's just not going to be tasty. Having more life experience, adults know that not only is it good but also good for them.

The world gives the idea to nonbelievers that God isn't worth a taste. The world emphasizes a self-focus, while the Lord says put others before self and God before all. In reality, walking and talking with God is the best thing you can do for yourself. As you walk with God, learning to pray and lean on Him and operate in His will, you are storing up treasures for yourself in heaven. In the world you are demonstrating the love of Christ and being an influence to get others to taste of the Lord.

Like so many foods that are good for us, all it requires is that first taste, a tiny morsel, which whets the appetite for more of Him. Then you can be open to all the goodness, all the fullness of the Lord.

Lord, fill my cup to overflowing with Your love, so that it pours out of me in a way that makes others want what I have. Amen.

The Right Focus

*Turning your ear to wisdom and applying your heart to understanding—
indeed, if you call out for insight and cry aloud for understanding, and if
you look for it as for silver and search for it as for hidden treasure, then you
will understand the fear of the LORD and find the knowledge of God.*

PROVERBS 2:2–5 NIV

. . . .

If you've ever lost something—your keys, your glasses, or an important document—you no doubt searched everywhere. Sometimes when you finally find it, you realize that, in your haste, you simply overlooked the very thing you were frantically searching for.

It comes down to focus. Even when you're looking in the right direction, you can still miss something because your focus is slightly off. This can be the challenge in our relationship with God. We can ask God a question and be really intent in getting the answer, only to find that His response to us was there all along—just not the answer we expected or wanted.

Frustration and stress can keep us from clearly seeing the things that God puts before us. Time spent in prayer and meditation on God's Word can often move day-to-day distractions out of the way and provide a clear picture of God's intentions for our lives. Step outside the pressure and into His presence, and get the right focus for whatever you're facing today.

Lord, help me to avoid distractions and keep my eyes on You. Amen.

Full Redemption and Love

*Israel, put your hope in the L*ORD*, for with the L*ORD *is*
unfailing love and with him is full redemption.
PSALM 130:7 NIV

. . . .

Jesus offers each of us full redemption: complete freedom from sin because of His great love for us. God doesn't want us to carry around our list of sins, being burdened by our past mistakes. He wants us to have a clear conscience, a joy-filled life!

The Bible tells us that God removes our sins as far as the east is from the west (Psalm 103:12) and that He remembers our sin no more (Isaiah 43:25, Hebrews 8:12). It's so important to confess your sins to the Lord as soon as you feel convicted and then turn from them and move in a right direction. There is no reason to hang your head in shame over sins of the past.

Turning from sin is tough. Especially when it has become a bad habit. Find an accountability partner to pray for you and check in with you about your struggles, but don't allow the devil to speak lies into your life. You have full redemption through Jesus Christ!

Dear Jesus, I confess my sin to You. Thank You for blotting out each mistake and not holding anything against me. Help me to make right choices through the power of Your Spirit inside me. Amen.

Pass It On!

After the usual readings from the books of Moses and the prophets,
those in charge of the service sent them this message: "Brothers, if you
have any word of encouragement for the people, come and give it."
ACTS 13:15 NLT

• •

Who doesn't need encouragement? After the reading in the temple, the rulers asked Paul and his companions if they had a word of encouragement to share. Paul immediately stood up and proclaimed how the fulfillment of God's promise came through Jesus; and whoever believed—whether Jew or Gentile—would receive forgiveness and salvation (Acts 13:16–41).

The scriptures state that as Paul and Barnabas left the synagogue, the people invited them to speak again the following Sabbath. And as a result of Paul's testimony, many devout Jews came to Christ. Not only that, on the next Sabbath, nearly the entire town—Jews and Gentiles alike—gathered to hear God's Word (Acts 13:42–44).

Encouragement brings hope. Have you ever received a word from someone that instantly lifted your spirit? Did you receive a bit of good news or something that diminished your negative outlook? Perhaps a particular conversation helped to bring your problems into perspective. Paul passed on encouragement and many benefited. So the next time you're encouraged, pass it on! You may never know how your words or actions benefited someone else.

Lord, thank You for the wellspring of encouragement
You give us through Your Holy Word. Amen.

Hang In There

Let perseverance finish its work so that you may be
mature and complete, not lacking anything.
JAMES 1:4 NIV

• •

Perseverance can't be rushed. The only way to develop perseverance is to endure challenges over a long period of time. A weightlifter must gradually add more weight to build muscle. A runner must run farther and farther, pushing past what is comfortable. If these athletes want to grow and improve, they must persevere through resistance over time.

The same is true for our faith. If we want to grow as Christians, we have to endure hard times. God allows difficult things into our lives to help build our strength and endurance. Just as the athlete who gives up at the first sign of hardship will never improve at her sport, the Christian who abandons her faith during times of distress will never reach maturity.

No one ever said the Christian life was an easy one. In fact, Christ told us we'd endure hardships of many kinds. But He also said not to get discouraged. When we stick it out and follow Him no matter what, we will become mature and complete, perfectly fulfilling God's plan for our lives.

Dear Father, help me to persevere when life gets hard.
Help me cling to You and do things Your way, even when it
feels like I can't go on. I trust that You won't give me more than
I can handle and You're working to make me mature. Amen.

Seek God

"I love all who love me. Those who search will surely find me."
PROVERBS 8:17 NLT

. . . .

Remember playing hide-and-seek as a child? Sometimes it was easy to find your sibling or friend. A foot sticking out from behind the couch or chair was a dead giveaway! Other times, a playmate may have selected a better hiding place. He was harder to find. You searched high and low. You looked behind doors and beneath beds. You lifted quilts and moved aside piles of pillows. But you didn't give up. Not until you found him!

Scripture tells us that God loves those who love Him and that if we search for Him, we will surely find Him. One translation of the Bible says it this way: "Those who seek me early and diligently shall find me" (AMPC).

Seek God in all things and in all ways. Search for Him in each moment of every day you are blessed to walk on this earth. He is found easily in His creation and in His Word. He is with you. Just look for Him. He wants to be found!

Father in heaven, thank You for Your unfailing
love for me. Help me to search for You diligently.
I know that when I seek, I will find You. Amen.

No matter HOW MANY TIMES WE FAIL, *no matter* HOW MANY TIMES WE MESS UP, *God won't write us off.*

Bringing Us to Completion

*Being confident of this, that he who began a good work in you
will carry it on to completion until the day of Christ Jesus.*
PHILIPPIANS 1:6 NIV

Remember the old saying "If at first you don't succeed, try, try again"? That's an encouraging statement. But it doesn't tell us how many times we should try. It doesn't tell us when we should throw in the towel and give up.

While there may be an appropriate time to give up on a certain skill or project, we should never give up on people. We should continue to hope, continue to pray, continue to love them. After all, that's what God does for us.

No matter how many times we fail, no matter how many times we mess up, God won't write us off. He's still working on us. He still loves us. He knows our potential, because He created us, and He won't stop moving us forward until His plan is completed.

Those of us who have been adopted into God's family through believing in His Son, Jesus Christ, can be confident that God won't give up on us. No matter how messed up our lives may seem, He will continue working in us until His plan is fulfilled, and we stand before Him, perfect and complete.

Dear Father, thank You for not giving up on
me. Help me to cooperate with Your process
of fulfilling Your purpose in me. Amen.

167

Teach Me Your Paths

Show me your ways, LORD, teach me your paths.
Guide me in your truth and teach me, for you are God
my Savior, and my hope is in you all day long.
PSALM 25:4–5 NIV

This psalm is a great prayer to memorize and keep close in your mind each day. The Bible tells us that God's Word is a lamp for your feet (Psalm 119:105). As you read, study, and let God's Word soak down in your heart, the Holy Spirit will bring those words to mind to guide you and show you the way that God wants you to go. If you want to hear God's voice and know His will for your life, get into His Word.

Hebrews 4:12 tells us that the scriptures are living and active. Just think about that for a moment. God's Word is alive! It can be difficult to find the time to open the Bible and meditate on the message—but it's *necessary* if you want God to teach you His path for your life.

Instead of giving up on finding time for Bible reading, get creative. Download a free Bible app on your phone. Sign up to have a daily scripture reading and devotion emailed to you. Jot down a few verses on a note card to memorize. There are many ways to get in the Word of God and be trained by it. Start today!

Lord, I believe Your Word is living and active. I want to
know Your will for my life. Help me get in Your Word
more and understand Your plan for me. Amen.

168

Love Made Perfect

There is no fear in love. But perfect love drives out fear,
because fear has to do with punishment. The one who fears is not
made perfect in love. We love because he first loved us.

1 JOHN 4:18–19 NIV

It's good to fear God, isn't it? God is awesome and fierce in His power. Yet, while we need to have a healthy respect for God, we don't need to be terrified of Him. At least, not if we really love Him.

Those who truly love God with all their hearts and souls have nothing to fear, for we know He loves us even more. We know that although He may allow us to walk through some difficult things, His plans for us are always good. When we love God, His love is made perfect in us. Our love for God causes His love for us to reign.

It's only when we choose not to love God that we need to fear Him, for though God's patience is long, He is a just God. He will not let the guilty go unpunished. When we love God with our lives, there's no need for punishment. When we love God with our lives, we love others and put their needs ahead of our own. And that, dear friends, is how His love is made perfect in us.

Dear Father, thank You for loving me. I want to love You
with my life and honor You with my actions. Amen.

Be Happy!

Blessed are those who act justly, who always do what is right.
PSALM 106:3 NIV

Did you know that the Greek word for *happy* is the same one for *blessed*? It sounds strange to us because we think *happy* refers to an emotional state. The truth is that neither of these words means anything emotional but instead talks about the recognition that everything good or fortunate that happens to us is a gift from God.

In the world that we live in today, some might think that a bank error or a mistake on a bill in their favor would be justification for keeping the money without a word. But a true Christ follower would not look at these kinds of situations as good or fortunate events. We would find happiness and blessedness in bringing such an error to the attention of the appropriate parties. Our happiness is being honest, doing what is right, because that happiness is the promised spiritual reward.

Because we want to be blessed by God, to be a happy follower of Him, we will seek to always do what is right.

Gracious and heavenly Father, thank You for Your blessings
each and every day. I am thankful to be Your follower.
When I am tempted to do something that would displease You,
remind me that You will bless me if I act justly. My happiness
will be a much better reward. In Your name, amen.

Your Heavenly Father

The LORD's love never ends; his mercies never stop.
They are new every morning; LORD, your loyalty is great.
LAMENTATIONS 3:22–23 NCV

. . . .

Because we live in a fallen world, relationships are far from perfect. Perhaps your relationship with your earthly father is wonderful, but it may be messy or fragmented. Take time today to celebrate your earthly father. Call your dad or, if you live close, spend some time with him. If it is within your power, seek to restore any brokenness in your relationship with your earthly father.

Regardless of your relationship with your earthly father, your heavenly Father loves you with an *unfailing love*. He is faithful to walk with you through the ups and downs of life. Remember that every day is a day to honor your heavenly Father. Begin and end today praising Him for who He is. Express thanksgiving. Present your requests to Him. Tell Him how much you love Him. God longs to be your Abba Father, a loving Daddy to you, His daughter!

Thank You that You are a loving God,
my Abba Father, my redeemer. Amen.

Building Trust

Trust in the LORD with all your heart and lean not on
your own understanding; in all your ways submit to
him, and he will make your paths straight.
PROVERBS 3:5–6 NIV

Many corporations take their executives to leadership training courses to develop better working relationships. Divided into teams, these people have to learn to trust one another. One favorite exercise is on the ropes course. A person is trussed up in a harness, steps off a tall tower, and is flung into a wide-open space, trusting his team members will guide him safely back to the ground. It takes a measure of courage to make yourself participate, but the results are usually exhilarating.

Placing our trust in a loving heavenly Father can sometimes feel like stepping off a precipice. Why? Perhaps it is because we can't see God. Trust is not easily attained. It comes once you have built a record with another over a period of time. It involves letting go and knowing you will be caught.

In order to trust God, we must step out in faith. Challenge yourself to trust God with one detail in your life each day. Build that trust pattern and watch Him work. He will not let you down. He holds you securely in His hand. He is your hope for the future.

Father, I release my hold on my life and trust in You. Amen.

Love Gone Cold

"Sin will be rampant everywhere, and the love of many will grow cold."
MATTHEW 24:12 NLT

. . . .

In a messed-up world that continually gives us advice contrary to what the Bible says, love and relationships get messed up too. When people become inconvenienced by their marriages and relationships, the common response today is to run. They stop showing love for each other and allow a cold heart to settle in.

God wants us to honor our commitments, and in doing so, we honor Him. Relationships take a lot of work. Marriage is a constant process of serving your husband, trusting and forgiving each other daily. Friendships take patience and understanding. Families need lots of love and grace.

When you allow love to grow cold in your relationships, you turn from God's will in your life. Our primary purpose on earth is to love the Lord and love others (Matthew 22:37–39). Even when it's tough or uncomfortable. Remember that love is a choice.

So when you feel love growing cold, pray for God's love to shine in your heart and warm up your relationships.

Heavenly Father, keep my love from growing cold.
Please give me the strength to keep loving when relationships
get difficult. Help me not to run the other way but to
keep my commitments and honor You. Amen.

New Believers

Then he said to his disciples, "The harvest is plentiful but the workers are few.
Ask the Lord of the harvest, therefore, to send out workers into his harvest field."
MATTHEW 9:37–38 NIV

. . . .

The Bible tells about a woman named Lydia who, unlike many women of her time, was a merchant. She sold expensive purple cloth. Lydia worshipped the true God of Israel, but she had not yet become a believer in Christ.

One day, Lydia and others gathered near a river just outside the city of Philippi. It was the Sabbath, and Paul and several of his companions were in town teaching the people about Jesus. They went down by the river and talked with the women there. While Lydia listened to them, God opened her heart to receive the message of Christ. Lydia believed and was baptized. Then she persuaded Paul and his companions to stay at her home for a while. This was the beginning of Lydia's service for the Lord. The Bible suggests that her home became a meeting place for believers.

Encouragement is important to new believers. When Lydia accepted Christ, she was eager to learn more about Him. Paul and his companions agreed to go to her home, where they encouraged her in her faith. Perhaps you know a new believer who could use your encouragement. Think of ways you can help them today.

Dear Lord, whom can I encourage today?
Show me a new believer who could use my help. Amen.

Start Your Day with God

In the morning, LORD, you hear my voice; in the morning
I lay my requests before you and wait expectantly.
PSALM 5:3 NIV

Mornings are hard for a lot of people—especially night owls who get more done in the evening. And verses like Psalm 5:3 can tend to make night owls feel like they aren't as spiritual as those who get up early to be with God.

The reality is that God wants to be the very center of your life. He doesn't want to be at the top of your priority list—just another box to check off each day. He wants your heart and attention morning, noon, and night. You won't get more points with God if you read ten Bible verses before your morning cup of coffee.

So how can you start your day with God even if you haven't gotten up hours earlier for devotions? As you wake up in the morning, thank the Lord for a new day. Ask Him to control your thoughts and attitude as you make the bed. Thank Him for providing for you as you toast your bagel. Ask that your self-image be based on your relationship with Christ as you get dressed and brush your teeth. Continue to pray as you drive to work or school. Spend time in His Word throughout the day. End your day by thanking Him for His love and faithfulness.

God wants a constant relationship with you, and He is available and waiting to do life with you twenty-four hours a day.

Dear Lord, thank You for the gift of a new day.
Help me be aware of Your constant presence in my life. Amen.

True Love

Love is patient, love is kind. It does not envy, it does not boast,
it is not proud. It does not dishonor others, it is not self-seeking,
it is not easily angered, it keeps no record of wrongs. Love does not
delight in evil but rejoices with the truth. It always protects,
always trusts, always hopes, always perseveres. Love never fails.
1 CORINTHIANS 13:4–8 NIV

Imagine the daunting task of accurately defining *love*. Most dictionaries rely on synonymous phrases: Love is "a strong affection," "a warm attachment," "a benevolent concern for others." Dictionaries define love through the language of emotion.

The apostle Paul understood that love is more than a feeling. When he sat down to write his famous description of love in 1 Corinthians 13:4–8, instead of defining the word *love*, he explained what love is—love is the demonstration of selfless acts toward others.

Paul explained that true love is displayed through the unselfish behaviors of patience, kindness, humility, forgiveness, protection, trust, hopefulness, and perseverance. This is the kind of love that Jesus showed toward others and that God shows toward us every day. God's kind of love never fails.

The words *I love you* slip easily from the lips and drift away. The passionate feeling of love sometimes grows cold. But God's love doesn't change. It is always pure, unconditional, and forever.

Heavenly Father, remind me of Paul's words
today. Help me to love others not only through my
words but also through my actions. Amen.

176

Rest for Your Soul

"Come to me, all you who are weary and burdened, and I will give you rest.
Take my yoke upon you and learn from me, for I am gentle and humble in heart,
and you will find rest for your souls. For my yoke is easy and my burden is light."
MATTHEW 11:28–30 NIV

Jesus says, "Come to Me." Just as He invited the little children to come to Him, Jesus calls us to come to Him and bring all of our burdens and lay them at His feet. He wants to help. He wants to relieve the load we're carrying.

A yoke is a harness placed over an animal or set of animals for the purpose of dragging something or carrying heavy equipment. Jesus liked to use visual imagery to get His meaning across. Can't you just picture all the burdens you are carrying right now strapped to your back like an ox plowing a field? Now imagine yourself unloading each one onto Jesus' shoulders instead. Take a deep breath.

Jesus tells us many times throughout the Gospels not to worry. Worrying about something will never help you. Worry makes things worse and burdens seem larger. Worry clutters up your soul. Jesus wants us to find rest in Him. Hear His gentle words rush over you—"Come to Me." Find rest for your soul.

Jesus, thank You for taking my burdens. I give them
fully to You. Help me not to take them back! I want
the rest and peace that You are offering. Amen.

He Won't Let You Down

I tell you that Christ has become a servant of the Jews on behalf of God's
truth, so that the promises made to the patriarchs might be confirmed.
ROMANS 15:8 NIV

Everyone has been hurt at one time or another by a broken promise. When that happens, it is best to forgive and go on. People are just people. They mess up. But there is one who will never break His promises to us—our heavenly Father. We can safely place our hope in Him.

Hebrews 11 lists Bible people who placed their trust and hope in God and weren't let down. Do you think Noah was excited about building an ark? Surely Sarah and Abraham hadn't planned on being elderly parents. Daniel faced the lions' den knowing his God would care for him. We can find encouragement from their examples, knowing that their faith in the God who'd come through for them time and again wasn't misplaced. They did not grow weary and lose heart. They knew He was always faithful.

Today we choose to place our hope in God's promises. We won't be discouraged by time—God's timing is always perfect. We won't be discouraged by circumstances—God can change everything in a heartbeat. We will keep our hearts in God's hand. For we know He is faithful.

Lord, I choose this day to place my trust in You.
I know You're the one, true constant in my life. Amen.

Lord,
I CHOOSE THIS
DAY TO PLACE MY
TRUST IN YOU.
I KNOW YOU'RE
THE ONE,
TRUE CONSTANT
IN MY LIFE.

Prayer and the Word Unlock the Door

I pray that your hearts will be flooded with light so that you can understand the confident hope he has given to those he called— his holy people who are his rich and glorious inheritance.

EPHESIANS 1:18 NLT

. . . .

Mathematics has a language all its own—a language that many students struggle to learn. Sometimes they never understand it completely but retain just enough of the language to make it through required courses. Some struggling students may need another person who speaks "math" to help them unlock the door to the language barrier.

God's ways are not the ways of this world, and sometimes matters of your spiritual journey may feel like they're in another language. Prayer can unlock the door to understanding God's Word and His design for your life. As you spend time with God in prayer asking for understanding of His Word, His truth will speak to you in a brand-new way. The Holy Spirit will help you unlock the secrets of His purpose and plan for your life.

Discovering His purpose for your life can be exciting, if you're willing to open the door to a new adventure with Him.

Heavenly Father, thank You for the Bible. Help me to read it with understanding and come to know You in a whole new way. Amen.

Hand Holders

As long as Moses held up his hands, the Israelites were winning, but whenever he lowered his hands, the Amalekites were winning. When Moses' hands grew tired, they took a stone and put it under him and he sat on it. Aaron and Hur held his hands up—one on one side, one on the other—so that his hands remained steady till sunset. So Joshua overcame the Amalekite army with the sword.

Exodus 17:11–13 NIV

How do you view your pastor? Do you see him as the cheerleader of your congregation, trying to motivate them to be better Christ followers? Perhaps the teacher? Maybe even the ultimate decision maker? The truth is some pastors feel that they are expected to be all things to all people and to do it with perfection.

Our verse today shows that Moses was an ordinary (but called) person trying to do a huge job by himself. No one could be expected to hold his hands up for the duration of a battle. He needed help. One way we can help our pastors in the work they have been given is by the power of consistent prayer for them personally, for their families, and for their ministry.

Father, our pastors are precious to us. Yet, we know
they have been given big assignments with sometimes
unrealistic expectations. Remind us to keep our pastors,
their families, and their ministry in prayer. It is one
way we can hold their hands high to You. Amen.

Praying for God's Will

For this reason, since the day we heard about you, we have not stopped praying for you. We continually ask God to fill you with the knowledge of his will through all the wisdom and understanding that the Spirit gives.

COLOSSIANS 1:9 NIV

The apostle Paul reminded the Colossians that he was continuously praying for them to be filled with the knowledge of God's will. Read Colossians 1:9 again. How did Paul ask God to fill them with the knowledge of His will? The only way that we can know His will—*through all the wisdom and understanding that the Spirit gives.* Paul was speaking to believers here. Christians have received the Holy Spirit as their counselor and guide. Those who do not have a personal relationship with Christ are lacking the Spirit, and thus, they are not able to discern God's will for their lives. Always take advantage of the wonderful gift that you have been given. If you have accepted Christ as your Savior, you also have the Spirit. One of the greatest things about the Holy Spirit is that He helps us to distinguish God's call on our life from the other voices of the world. Pray that God will reveal His good and perfect will for your life. His Holy Spirit at work in you will never lead you down a wrong path.

God, help me to draw upon the wonderful resource
that I have as a Christian. Help me, through the power
of the Holy Spirit, to know Your will. Amen.

How to Love

My children, we should love people not only with words
and talk, but by our actions and true caring.
1 JOHN 3:18 NCV

. . . .

We've often heard the phrase "Talk is cheap."

Of course, that phrase doesn't refer to money, does it? It's a reminder that while anyone can *say* they care about starving children, few will shell out the cash to actually feed them. While anyone can *say* they care about our current political climate, few will actually take the time to try to change things for the better. And when we're in a crisis, many people may *say* they care about us. But how many people will sit with us in the middle of the night because we're still not over the loved one we lost six months ago?

Not many.

It's easy to tell people we care about them. But God wants more from us than our words. Sometimes compassionate words and a prayer are all we can offer, but when that's the case, we need to make sure we do pray. And when it is in our ability to do more, we need to put action to our words. Do we really care about that teenage girl with low self-esteem? Don't just tell her she's beautiful and leave her with her dated, faded clothes. Buy her a new outfit.

Let's look for ways today that we can love those around us with our actions.

Dear Father, teach me to love like You love. Amen.

Prayer Touches God

*He was a devout, God-fearing man.... He gave generously
to the poor and prayed regularly to God.*
ACTS 10:2 NLT

In the book of Acts, a centurion named Cornelius received a vision from God. Though a Gentile, this man loved God, praying and fasting regularly. While he prayed, an angel of the Lord told Cornelius that God heard and honored his prayers. Accordingly, God instructed the centurion to go talk to Peter, God's servant.

Peter, having received a vision that God would cleanse and accept anyone whom the Jews deemed "unclean," agreed to meet this Gentile despite Jewish law. Cornelius invited his Gentile neighbors, friends, and family members when he met Peter in Caesarea. Realizing God orchestrated the meeting, Peter preached the gospel to Cornelius and all who joined him, and the entire group of Gentiles received the Holy Spirit (Acts 10:44–48).

Jesus takes note of a praying, giving heart like Cornelius had. Denominations mean little, while a contrite, teachable spirit touches God. Cornelius was a good, God-fearing man who needed to hear about salvation through Christ. So God honored his prayers and led him to the preacher— while teaching the preacher a thing or two at the same time.

Have you hesitated to share your faith with someone you think unseemly or beyond your realm of comfort? Begin now. Look what happened when Peter did.

Father, forgive me for my self-righteousness.
Open the way for me to witness to whomever You
have prepared to hear the gospel. Amen.

Time to Love God

*Do not forget this one thing, dear friends: With the Lord a day is
like a thousand years, and a thousand years are like a day.*

2 PETER 3:8 NIV

. . . .

"The time is just flying by."
  "I don't have time."
  "There aren't enough hours in a day."
  Surely you've heard those words. You've probably said them yourself.
In today's busy world, there just doesn't seem to be enough time. People
communicate instantaneously. They work quickly, play fast, and live by
tight schedules. Even when they pray, they expect God to answer quickly.
But God doesn't work that way. The Bible says that to Him a thousand years
are like a day.

God's patience with us is a reflection of His love. There are many
examples of His loving patience in the Bible, but the best is His patience
with the Israelites. Psalm 78:41 says, "Again and again they tested God's
patience" (NLT). Still, God continued to love them, and His patience with
Israel exists to this day.

Patience requires time, and although it is not infinite, God's patience is
immense. He allows people time to know Him, to trust Him, and to believe
in His Son and the gift of salvation. He gives them a lifetime in which to
do it and, after that, the promise of eternal life with Him in heaven. Now,
that's true love!

Dear God, help me to love others patiently,
the same way that You love me. Amen.

Be Joyful Despite It All

A twinkle in the eye means joy in the heart,
and good news makes you feel fit as a fiddle.
PROVERBS 15:30 MSG

The apostle Paul had much he could've grumbled about. He was beaten, jailed, shipwrecked, and nearly drowned; yet through it all, he discovered God was the source of his contentment. Paul understood God was in control of his life, even when he was in those overwhelming, tragic situations. Remember his songs of praise from the jail cell (Acts 16)?

Sometimes we find ourselves in hard places, and life isn't going the way we planned. This is the time we have to look for the positive. We have to make the choice to "bloom where we're planted," and God will meet us there. In our songs of praise amid the difficulties, God will come. The Holy Spirit, the comforter, will minister to our needs. The Lord has promised to never leave or forsake us, so if He is present, we should have no fear or worry. Without fear or worry, we can learn to be content. No fretting, no regretting, just trusting the Word is truth.

When we place our hope in Christ and He's our guide, He will give us the ability to walk satisfied, no matter our circumstances. He is our all in all.

Lord, I give You thanks for all Your good gifts
but most of all for Your presence. Amen.

Fix Your Thoughts on Truth

And now, dear brothers and sisters, one final thing. Fix your thoughts
on what is true, and honorable, and right, and pure, and lovely,
and admirable. Think about things that are excellent and worthy of praise.
PHILIPPIANS 4:8 NLT

In a world loaded with mixed messages and immorality of every kind, it becomes increasingly difficult to have pure thoughts and clear minds. What can a believer do to keep her mind set on Christ? Replace the negative message with a positive message from God's Word.

Think about the negative messages that you struggle with the most. Maybe you struggle with some of these: You're not thin enough. You're not spiritual enough. You've made a lot of mistakes, etc.

Dig through the scriptures and find truth from God's Word to combat the false message that you're struggling with. Write the passages down and memorize them. Here are a few to get you started:

God looks at my heart, not my outward appearance. (1 Samuel 16:7)

I am free in Christ. (1 Corinthians 1:30)

I am a new creation. My old self is gone! (2 Corinthians 5:17)

The next time you feel negativity and false messages slip into your thinking, fix your thoughts on what you know to be true. Pray for the Lord to replace the doubts and negativity with His words of truth.

Lord God, please control my thoughts and help me
set my mind and heart on You alone. Amen.

Relax

"You will not have to fight this battle. Take up your positions; stand firm and see the deliverance the LORD will give you."

2 CHRONICLES 20:17 NIV

Why do we always feel we need to fight our own battles?

Oh, God wants us to use common sense and stand up for others and ourselves when it's appropriate. But sometimes, it's best not to defend ourselves at all. Sometimes, when we know we've done no wrong, when we know we stand innocent before God in whatever situation we find ourselves, it's good just to remain still and calm and let God be our defender.

Truly, the more we defend ourselves, the guiltier we sound sometimes. But when we can stand before God with clean hands and a pure heart, God will deliver us. Oh, it may not be in the way we want. It may not happen as quickly as we'd like. But when we decide to stand firm, to continue living godly lives, to continue seeking His approval in our words, thoughts, and actions, we can trust Him.

Let's remember today to rest in His goodness, despite the battles that rage around us. We don't have to live our lives fighting. We can relax. Our Father is the judge, and He will deliver us.

Dear Father, thank You for being my defender.
Thank You for delivering me from all sorts of trouble.
Help me to relax and let You take care of me. Amen.

Keeping Quiet

Hatred stirs up conflict, but love covers over all wrongs.
PROVERBS 10:12 NIV

Let's face it. We all enjoy a juicy bit of gossip now and then. As wrong as that seems, most of us are guilty of stirring the pot at one time or another. It's not the worst thing we can do, right?

But God's Word tells us that gossip is more indicative of hatred than love. Words can do more damage than any amount of physical harm. Gossip hurts. It tears down and wounds our spirits. It causes deep pain, which can take years to heal. And sometimes its wounds never heal on this side of heaven.

Love always protects, always heals, always builds up. Sometimes, it's necessary to reveal hurtful information. But more often, we can just let things go and protect those around us from hurtful comments. We can keep our mouths shut, quit stirring the pot, and let conflicts die before they begin. Or at least, we can choose not to contribute to the conflict.

Hatred fans the flames of controversy and dissension without concern for who is hurt. Love, on the other hand, covers over wrongs. When love is exercised, conflict can be smothered before the damage gets out of control.

Dear Father, I want to build others up, not tear them
down. Forgive me for stirring up conflict. Help me
to show wisdom and love by refusing to contribute
to gossip, controversy, and dissension. Amen.

Your love, LORD,
reaches to
the heavens,
your faithfulness
to the skies.

PSALM 36:5 NIV

Love without Limits

Your love, LORD, reaches to the heavens, your faithfulness to the skies.
PSALM 36:5 NIV

. . . .

God's love and faithfulness have no bounds. They reach to the heavens. They stretch to the skies and beyond. This is hard for us to understand. As humans, even our very best attempts at love and faithfulness are limited. God's love is limitless. When God created you, knit you together in your mother's womb, and brought you into this world, He loved you. He loves you just as much today as He did when you were an innocent babe. He is incapable of loving you any less or any more than He already does. His love is not based on what you do or don't do. It is not here today and gone tomorrow due to any mistake or failure in your life. He is faithful even when we are faithless. If it seems that you are not close to God as you once were, He is not the one who moved. Draw close to your heavenly Father. You will find that He is there, faithful and true, ready to receive you back unto Himself. Thank the Lord today for an unfailing, unfathomable sort of love. What a blessing is the love of our faithful God!

Thank You, God, for loving me with a love that
reaches to the heavens. You are faithful even
when I am not. I love You, Lord. Amen.

A Declaration of Dependence

*"Sacrifice thank offerings to God, fulfill your vows to the Most High,
and call on me in the day of trouble; I will deliver you, and you will honor me."*
Psalm 50:14–15 niv

. . . .

Most of us value our relationships, whether they are with family, friends, or coworkers. We like being in relationships with those who offer love, commitment, and trust because we feel valued. Perhaps not so ironically, today's verse reveals that God wants the same things from us. He wants thankful, trusting, and faithful children, people whom He can delight in and who can delight in Him.

As our heavenly Father, He wants to help us, especially in times of trouble. That dependence on Him recognizes that everything we have comes from Him. The practical way to depend on Him comes through an honest, consistent lifestyle of prayer, where we offer ourselves and our needs. Through prayer, we draw near to Him and get to know Him better. In doing that, we'll become the thankful, trusting, and faithful children He desires.

Gracious and generous Father, thank You for loving me so much that You are interested in every facet of my life. I commit to bring everything to You in prayer and acknowledge that I am dependent on You for my provision and safety. I pray for the continued outpouring of Your Spirit in me, so I can ask for continued blessings for myself as well as others. I love You, Lord. Amen.